The Colour of Bendigo

A SHORT MULTICULTURAL HISTORY

Bill Clyde

Bendigo, Australia

Bill Clyde C/- Intertype Publish and Print
Unit 45, 125 Highbury Road
BURWOOD VIC 3125
www.intertype.com.au

Ordering Information:
Quantity sales. Special discounts are available on quantity purchases by corporations, associations, and others. For details, contact the "Special Sales Department" at the address above.

The Colour of Bendigo/ Bill Clyde. —1st ed.
ISBN 978-0-6455754-4-6

Contents

This book is dedicated to -

Bunjil

Dja Dja Wurrung People

Taungurung People

And the Oneness of all Humanity

FORWARD

When we talk about culture, we are using a term to describe ourselves both individually and collectively. It helps us to define and understand our identity within the greater world outside of ourselves. As a general rule of thumb, culture can be defined as including language, customs, history, food, religion, clothing, the arts, recreation and even the environment to which we belong. Certainly, culture can be a lot more than this. It does show us, on a global scale, the great diversity of human experience.

This book is intended to be a snapshot of the people who have made Bendigo home, both past and present. To give a detailed account of every culture ever present in Bendigo would run into a multi-volume work!

The idea for a multicultural history of Bendigo and the title came from Dr Arthur Chiang. All information presented and opinions expressed are mine and may not necessarily be endorsed by the good doctor.

Bill Clyde

CHAPTER ONE

DJAARA DREAMING

In a time before time, the Dja Dja Wurrung appeared in the country now known as the City of Greater Bendigo. According to traditional lore, Martinga Kulinga Murrup (Ancestral Spirits) gave Bunjil authority to shape Djandak (Country), raising plants from the soil, creating rivers and creeks, establishing ancient songlines and finally bringing people into creation. Every rock, plant, place, animal and water course was imbued with Murrups (Spirits), the land itself a complete living entity.

When finished, Bunjil became the Wedge Tailed Eagle and enlisted the help of Waa, the Crow, to create a system whereby the people could be born into either eagle or crow lineage and therefore be unrelated. Waa was thought to be originally white in colour, being burnt black when it bought fire back to earth.

Modern archaeology would suggest that the Dja Dja Wurrung and other First Nation peoples were part of a great migration, an extremely long time ago. This could have entailed walking south along a land bridge from South East Asia, possibly combined with one of humanity's earliest sea voyages. Whatever the case, our First Nation People have been on country a very long time.

The Dja Dja Wurrung people were originally made up from as many as sixteen to twenty-four clans, with many dialects thrown in for good measure. The word "Djaara" means people, which also identifies the Dja Dja Wurrung family – Dja Dja Wurrung being the language commonly used. Our

First Nation People were one of five tribes that made up the Kulin Nation in what would later be called Victoria.

Djarra Country

Djaara Country extends well beyond the boundary of the City of Greater Bendigo. To the east of Bendigo, we can trace Country up to Rochester, then over to Boort, taking in Donald, heading towards and easily accommodating St Arnaud, taking in most of the Kara Kara State Park, heading south to Mt Lonarch, across to Creswick, running south of, and including, Daylesford, up to Woodend and running northwards towards Redesdale, up to Rochester, completing the boundary.

The City of Bendigo encroaches the Country of the Taungurung People, which includes Lake Eppalock and Heathcote.

Dja Dja Wurrung Country, enormous in size, offered First Nation people an abundance of geographical features, many with ancient ceremonial significance. It provided water courses, fish, animal and plant species as food and medicine. On the hop were plentiful numbers of Gurri (Kangaroo) and Djinbong–gurri (Wallabies). Baramul (Emu) roamed both the forests and plains, with the water courses alive with an array of freshwater species.

Honey was readily available from the hives of the Mumumbarra (Bee) – quite easy to collect given that the local native bees don't sting!

The great forests of Yirrip (Ironbark) and Buludj (Box Eucalyptus) provided an array of materials for building Willams (huts), fashioning Datim datim (Boomerang) and Mulka (shields).

A very sweet beverage, known as Yerrip Korr, was made by soaking blossoms of the Ironbark tree in bowls made from the knobs and elbows of the trees. Long oval-shaped yams, eaten after roasting, had a sweet nutty flavour.

Long, thick cloaks made from possum skins provided warmth during the many cold months of winter. Spears, axes and stone knives were created and often traded with other First Nation people. When members of one tribe needed to enter another's Country, say for trading purposes, a ceremony call Tanderrum would be held. This was effectively a diplomatic ceremony, meaning "freedom of the bush".

Along with songlines, ancient ceremonies, dance and song, the Djaara people created art on rock and bark. Most importantly, they had a strong cultural understanding that Country owned them. They were spiritually connected to Country, just as Country was spiritually connected to them. Every activity, whether hunting or using ancient land management techniques, was bound to this oneness with Country.

The idea of occupying another's Country for themselves was something beyond First Nation concepts of living and being. After many millennia of living in a stable and culturally rich society, the Dja Dja Wurrung people had little idea of the shattering that was about to commence, changing their way of life forever.

CHAPTER TWO

INVASION

The southern clans of the Dja Dja Wurrung were probably the first to hear of the arrival of the strangers to the south. The Wurundjeri/Woi Wurrung people would have been astonished by the sight of very pale, strangely clothed Europeans. From what is now Tasmania, the first members of the Port Phillip Association disembarked, and the lives of the First Nation people would change forever.

In the book "Aboriginal Victorians" by Richard Broome, it is apparent that the original bush telegraph worked extremely well. It was noted by the early European arrivals that groups of natives would proceed to the settlement, largely to see these strange new people. Some were thought to have come "from the north". Initial contact appears to have been quite friendly, with exchanges of goods between the groups. The First Nation people of the southern clans were pleased with the gifts of flour and the new type of meat offered by the Europeans.

The Port Phillip Association, its arrival not condoned by the Colonial Government or the local owners, had one great purpose in mind – open up southern New South Wales to sheep. The woollen mills of England seemed to have an insatiable thirst for Antipodean wool. The Europeans, mostly from the British Isles, were here to stay.

John Batman, to some credit, did try to organise a legal "sale" or treaty to purchase 200,000 hectares of land and did obtain "signatures" of tribal elders in exchange for many gifts. However, it is extremely unlikely that the elders knew what they were actually doing, given that buying and selling of country would have been completely alien to their cultural connections and beliefs. Incidentally, this would be the only time any sort of agreement between First Nations and Europeans would be sought until far more recent times.

When the Governor in Sydney heard about this "purchase", he took immediate steps to void the document. Governor Richard Bourke would issue a Proclamation declaring all land to be "Terra Nullius", that the Aboriginal people had no ownership rights whatsoever, with all land belonging to the Crown.

The first known incursion into Dja Dja Wurrung country by Europeans occurred in 1836. The expedition led by Major Thomas Mitchell had set out from Sydney to explore what was for them unknown territory. Going to the top of a mountain he named Mt Byng, Mitchell looked north and proclaimed the country "Australia Felix" which roughly translates as fortunate or lucky Australia. The mountain, by the way, already had a name – Leanganook – which translates as "large shoulders" (supporting the head of ceremony). Travelling through country in late winter/early spring, Mitchell was very impressed with the water filled creeks and splendid greenery. In his British mindset, he thought that Providence had left it to Englishmen to settle and cultivate.

One important aspect of British culture at the time, shared by a number of European countries, was what we might call the "Culture of Empire". Fundamentally, this cultural mindset was founded upon ideas of superiority – racial, religious, structural and historical pre-eminence. Apart from Britain, France, Spain, Portugal, Holland and Austria/Hungary had empires too. We should remember that empire building was not just a European mindset, given the Ottoman Turks had had a great empire, let alone the Mongols of centuries before. Like any quest for Empire, it would mean the use of force to subjugate whole populations of people and enforce new cultural norms upon them – the cultural norms of the conquerors. Ultimately, the quest for Empire would bring conflict within empires and conflict between empires.

The Dja Dja Wurrung faced a two-pronged incursion into Country in 1838 – from both north and south. According to the new law of the land, the pastoralists (also known as squatters) would venture into the "new" territories, select a huge parcel of land and then apply to the Government in Sydney for a lease. The pastoralists would then return with their servants – many of whom were ticket of leave convicts – and vast flocks of sheep. Although Mitchell has described an immense green and well watered Australia Felix, the year 1838 and 1839 proved to be drought years – giving the pastoralists a massive jolt to their money making ideas.

In the spirit of keeping this book about Bendigo, we shall keep our focus on events that occurred in, or very close to, the current municipal boundary. That is not to diminish what occurred elsewhere in Dja Dja Wurrung country, or anywhere else for that matter.

In 1838, Captain Charles Hutton arrived in the Campaspe area, having arrived with his sheep and servants from Yass. They had experienced hostility from the "river tribes" of the Goulburn Valley who appeared to have resisted the invasion of their lands. This run was given the name "Campaspe Plains".

In 1839 Henry Grey Bennett established the 'Barnedown Run', a creek would flow through the run that would eventually carry the name Bendigo Creek. Bennett's sheep would graze high up the Bendigo Valley with an outstation, which is a nice way of naming a shepherd's hut, in the vicinity of the Shamrock Hotel.

The renamed Leanganook (Mt Byng), Mt Alexander, would have a number of pastoralists claim a part of it, Richard Grice being the largest leasee. Along with Charles Sherratt, Grice would establish the 'Mount Alexander North Run', which included the southern part of the Bendigo Valley. The intention was very clear – the original locals were to make way for the pastoralists and their flocks of sheep. The First Nation people were seen as savages, without any rights as understood in the European mindset. What was sacred, living country to the Dja Dja Wurrung people, was merely a resource to be utilised for the personal gain of the largely middle-class pastoralists. Not so worthy as to be called by their traditional group names, the First Nation peoples would be termed 'the blacks' by those of much fairer skin.

The new arrivals erected small bark huts not unlike those of the original inhabitants. One might wonder what the middle class pastoralists thought of their very basic, daily menu of unleavened bread (damper), mutton and black tea made from what local water could be sourced. The First Nation people quickly became accustomed to receiving rations from the pastoralists and along with a new practice called smoking, the slow break-up on their traditional way of life began.

Certainly, many First Nation people began a resistance to the newcomers. This was fuelled by European servants mistreating local original people, including sexual assaults upon women. Captain Hutton had forcibly run-off Djaara People from the run after his arrival in 1838. Most contemporary accounts give a view that most Dja Dja Wurrung people seemed to accept the rather horrific new reality presented to them. Some would directly experience just how horrific the new reality was.

The years 1838 and 1839 would see armed attacks upon First Nation people, the ferocity of such causing an outcry that made Hutton sell the lease in 1840. The main thing is that one culture, uninvited and armed, would violently subjugate the existing culture for reasons of personal profit and extending the notion and culture of Empire.

After Hutton's arrival, five Dja Dja Wurrung were killed by some of Hutton's servants. In what appears to have been a reprisal attack, a hutkeeper and shepherd were killed with 700 sheep run off. The assailants were believed to have been "Goulburn River" tribes, which would imply Taungurung tribes. The name Daung Wurrung is often used here too. Hutton collected a party of servants and attacked a group at the Coliban River near present day Lake Eppalock. Hutton would later state that as many as 40 were killed. That those who were killed and wounded were probably not the ones responsible for the deaths of the servants seemed to be of no consequence to Hutton. Later Hutton and a party of mounted police would attack a group of Djaara People, killing at least six with many wounded. It is known that in both instances the First Nation people did put up a spirited but ineffectual defence with spears. The Europeans were just out of spear range; however, the original inhabitants were within rifle range. Across Djaara Country (and the whole continent), there would be other shootings and poisonings of First Nation people.

The point was made very clear – the "savages", their culture, their land, their ways, would have to be surrendered to the Europeans, who, by the way, considered themselves to be far more "civilised" than those they had forcibly deposed. The invasion was now a permanent occupation.

As an act of mercy, the British Parliament established an Aboriginal Protectorate system in the Port Phillip district, which began operating in 1839. There would be four Assistant Protectors, headed by Chief Protector George Robinson. Djaara Country, which was by then called the Loddon or North Western District, came under the control of Assistant Protector Edward Parker. The original people would be referred to as the Loddon Tribes, Campaspe Tribes, Coliban Blacks and so forth. The use of "Blacks" or "Tribes" depended on who you were talking to.

The Protectors did try to investigate the reported shootings of First Nation people, along with other accounts of mistreatment. Both Robinson and Parker investigated the shootings at Campaspe Plains, both being quite outraged at what had happened and the overall attitude of Hutton towards the original owners. Hutton's attitudes and actions might be classified as ethnic cleansing in today's terminology, if not outright genocide.

Hutton and his servants, like most of those who committed such acts, were never charged or brought to account. The First Nation people were regarded as Heathens, amongst other things, and they could not give a legal testimony in any form. As mentioned previously, Hutton faced considerable condemnation, selling his run in 1840 and buying another near present day Yea.

The Protectors would establish "stations" which were settlements designed to bring tribes together, offering official protection from harm and also beginning the process of "civilising" them. Edward Parker would attempt establishing stations at Jackson Creek and Tarrengower Hill, before finally deciding on an area on the northern side of Mt Franklin. The station would encompass a creek, later known as Jim Crow Creek. Parker called the station Franklinford, establishing it in June 1841. Possibly as many as 400 Dja Dja Wurrung people would accompany Parker to this sanctuary. Certainly, many more Djaara People would still choose to live in their traditional areas, despite the real threat from Europeans.

Those in the Protectorate station were dressed in European clothing and given simple Christian instruction. A schoolhouse would provide the British 3 "R's", reading (w)riting and (a)rithmetic to the children. Plots of land were made available for the Djaara to learn farming – which would have been quite a cultural shock for them. Indeed, everything since the incursion of the Europeans had been a massive and unpleasant shock to them. Despite this, they still continued to practice ancient ceremonies, keeping the core of their culture alive. It is known that in November 1843, the Djaara People would create a 6 metre snake from bark, holding a corroboree for Mindye (or Mindi), the Giant Serpent.

All seemed well for a little while, however that did not last. The year 1843 would see the beginnings of a decline in government funding for the Protectorate system. Some Djaara people at Franklinford decided to rejoin those still clinging to a new embattled traditional way of life. Djaara people had little resistance to diseases that they had not traditionally known – measles and chicken pox for example. The Europeans had also brought with them their drug of choice – alcohol.

On the last day of the year 1848, the Protectorate system was wound up. Parker and his family would stay on at Franklinford, with some of the remaining Dja Dja Wurrung people (about 30 or 40), deciding to remain there as well. The schoolhouse and other buildings fell into disrepair and many farms were left abandoned. In 1864, 31 adults and 6 children were at Franklinford, some being forcibly resettled at Coranderrk Station, Badger's Creek, Healesville.

The early pastoralists were quick to make a fortune and as quick to sell their leases. Some of the pastoral runs would change hands 3, 4 or 5 times between 1837 and 1850. I assume that many probably felt the huge cultural shock of being away from their familiar environs and thrust into which might be called a frontier society. The original bark huts they built – Mia Mias as they usually called them – gave way to larger, although not overly large, more solid structures. From Bendigo Valley, it was a week's walk to Melbourne. The niceties of British life were quite hard to transport over the hills and dales in between.

The flocks of sheep grew rapidly along with increasing numbers of cattle and horses grazing on the land once roamed by the Dja Dja Wurrung people. The "kings in grass castles" seemed eternally set on their almost Baronial rule over the lands now conquered. They rejoiced in the decision made in Sydney in early 1851– the Port Philip District would become the Colony of Victoria, with its own governor and an elected House of Parliament that they could vote for. Little did they know, as the Colony of Victoria came into being, that they too would experience what it would be like to have their lands and their way of life shattered beyond all recognition.

CHAPTER THREE

FEVER

The Dja Dja Wurrung people had little need for the shining, golden-yellow rocks that peppered much of their country. To other people, this country was literally a pot of gold waiting to be exploited for their own wealth.

Much of the Bendigo region had once been an ancient seabed – the layers of various sedimentary sandstone and slate bearing testament to this long drawn out process. One layer was so unique, it was termed the Bendigo Strata, perhaps the only strata to be given a name by its official human area of habitation. Over eons the seabed rose, with volcanic eruptions creating what is now known as the Great Dividing Range – spreading lava far and wide, cooling as granite or basalt, sometimes with quartz thrown in for good measure. A period of folding (mountain building) would continue, bringing quartz intrusions much closer to the surface, sometimes breaching it. Gold being a metal, found its way into the mix of the still molten quartz, and cooling as its host rock did so too. Mighty quartz outcrops occasionally rose above the surface soil, speckled with golden nuggets. One such outcrop – Specimen Hill – was a place of special significance to the Dja Dja Wurrung people. No need to go looking for it now as it was obliterated one and a half centuries ago for the gold it contained.

Frederick Fenton was now the owner of the run that was once the Mt Alexander North run. It was called "Ravenswood", a name from the novel "Bride of Lammermoor" by Sir Walter Scott. The 'Anglofication' of Country

was well underway. The creek in the northern part of the run had been giv-
en the name "Bendigo Creek" after one of the station hands who was handy
with his fists. James Mouat had been given the name "Bendigo" by other
station hands in honour of William Abednego Thompson, boxing champion
of Britain.

Gold had been found prior to Victoria becoming a colony but it was later
that the great discoveries were made. As Melbourne and the runs started to
clear of men eager to make their fortunes, news of gold at Mt Alexander
and then Bendigo Creek reached Melbourne. The pastoralists, who now
were usually referred to as squatters, found their runs over-run by gold
seekers who couldn't care less about their sheep runs. In the second half of
1851, little did the reasonably small population of mostly British people realise that a big chunk of the world would soon begin arriving in the "brand
new" British Colony.

To give you an idea of how immense this influx of people was, here are
some statistics from the Melbourne Immigration Museum. In 1835, the continent was believed to have a population of 279,148 people. The new settlement of Port Phillip numbered a couple of hundred. It should be noted
that the First Nation people were not included in the population statistics
until after 1967. In 1846, the population of Port Phillip would number
32,879, with one passenger ship arriving each week. Within four years of
gold discoveries (1855), the continental population would soar to 793,260
with Victoria's population at 347,305. More than a tenfold increase in nine
years, with nearly half of the population of Australia in Victoria. By 1865, the
Australian population was put at 1,309,043 with 617,791 living in Victoria.
Subsequent waves of immigration in the twentieth and twenty first centuries pale into insignificance compared to what took place between 1846 and
1865.

A great multicultural experience was now underway, not that anyone really sat down to analyse it. Europe had seen great conflict over the centuries
with more conflict to come. There would also be an influx of non-Europeans
too – the first time that many diverse cultural groups would come together,
face to face and either stand together or tear themselves apart. For the

scope of this book, we shall focus on Bendigo with a glimpse at what was happening a little further afield.

The story of the gold rushes is well known – initial rough living, with many being rewarded with considerable amounts of gold. Some Dja Dja Wurrung people also took up prospecting, mainly around Bullock Creek. Others would find employment on the squatters runs, now devoid of their European farm hands. The great damage caused by surface mining, and later deep lead sinking of mines, might have caused some distress to some of the First Nation people. Today's Dja Dja Wurrung see the land as still healing from the effects of that rush for fortune.

We will have a look at some of the people who came to Bendigo in those roaring , heady days, remembering that it might have been the first time someone from Cornwall, or Scotland, or Prussia, or France, or Italy, or China, ever came face to face with these people and their diverse cultures.

Walking around Bendigo today, one might think that it was all an enclave of Irish and Chinese people. There is a collection of operating and formerly operating hotels with Irish names and it is hard to miss the Chinese footprint in the Dragon City. By the late 1850's, the Irish and Chinese come second and third in the population stakes, number one position being held by the Cornish – "Cousin Jacks" to their friends.

Cornwall, which is located at the south western tip of England, is regarded as a province or area of England itself. However, it has ancient linkages that set it apart from most other shires of England. The Cornish language was quite distinct from the Gaelic spoken in most other shires of England. Long thought extinct, remnants of the language still survive, although limited to around 800 words. The Cornish themselves had a well-earned reputation for mining – tin mining was well established in Cornwall centuries ago. At the time of the gold discoveries in Victoria, Cornish immigrants were already mining tin in South Australia – their expertise would be invaluable to other gold seekers who had very little idea about mining at all. The Cornish were known for their pastry – or pasty, traditionally known as a "Tiddy Oggy". There would be variations with the name along with the ingredients. Usually filled with a mix of meat and vegetables wrapped in a solid pastry, this baked pasty provided a reasonable meal – the mining version often had meat and vegetables at one end, with stewed fruit at the other. According to traditional lore, the pasty could be heated on a shovel held over a candle. I should think that this would have taken considerable time. Pundits would say that the genuine Cornish pasty has crimping along the top, however crimping along the side is common which give the pasty its shape.

Most Cornish people were Methodist Christians, which meant they abstained from alcohol, gambling and (for the most conservative) from dancing as well. These were regarded as "sins" enflaming the passions to the point where even greater sinning might take place. In the twentieth century, some would avoid going to see motion pictures, such was their bent to beat temptation. In a sense, this alienated them to some degree from the bulk of the mixed goldfields population, given the proliferation of hotels that sprang up like mushrooms in the Autumn.

I wish to state at this point that I have maternal Cornish heritage, but fortunately from the line of the drinking Cornish fraternity! Although the Cornish were sprinkled throughout Bendigo, many would congregate in Long Gully, giving it the nickname "Little Cornwall".

The Irish people had already gone through some very tragic times in the late 1840's. Famine had taken 25% of the population with another 25% emigrating to avoid death from starvation. Most Irish were Roman Catholic Christians, many with a desire to see Ireland be rid of English-Protestant rule. The Northern Irish were usually fiercely Protestant Christians, mainly Church of England/Ireland or Presbyterian, who remained loyal to the English Crown. Many of the Northerners had Scottish heritage, although they adopted some of the wonderful traditions of the South. I claim paternal heritage from the people "up north".

Whether from the north or south, the Irish had a reputation for liking a drink or three – many would become publicans, leaving us a legacy of the Shamrock Hotel, the Limerick and Hibernian Hotels all still standing in central Bendigo. They bought the actual shamrock to Bendigo, which still flowers here and there across the suburbs. A member of the oxalis species, the squat, pink flowering, large three leaf plant, was bound to images of home and religion. It is said that the Patron Saint of Ireland, St Patrick, used the leaf of the shamrock to explain the Holy Trinity of Father, Son and Holy

Spirit. Another member of the introduced oxalis species, the vastly invasive yellow flowering "Sour grass", is common throughout the region and is extremely difficult to control.

Like the other nationalities on the goldfields, the Irish would mix with the other people during the day and congregate together at night. The area between the Central Business District and the Tramway Depot would be known as "Irishtown" although Irish people were dispersed throughout the entire region. Inventors of the bagpipes, they would have their musical instrument altered by the Scots, making some think that it was they who has devised this distinctive, wailing, yet melodic wind instrument way back in the mists of Highland time.

The Scots themselves made the bagpipes their own. Certainly, the sound of a highland pipe band can be quite stirring to those of non-Scottish background. Like their cousins the Irish, the Scots would claim Celtic ancestry although the earlier Scottish language became extinct after being superseded by Gaelic – a remnant of the invasion of Scotland by the Irish Gaels. There would have been Gaelic speakers in early Bendigo, although English was the official language of both countries. Both had tartans – a series of colourful designs which would denote a particular Clan, or association/affiliation with a clan. The Scots were quite distinctive in their love of, perhaps even reverence to, a particular concoction that has almost mythic proportions throughout the Western World! I am talking about the Haggis, which is, for some, an acquired taste they can never really acquire. Simply, a sheep's stomach stuffed with organs (including lung) and served hot – a mouthful of Haggis followed by a wee dram of whiskey is the traditional serving method. More formal settings would see a bagpiper playing ahead of the Haggis, announcing the triumphant arrival of this unusual tasty treat. Incidentally, the Scots invented golf.

The Welsh never invented anything as exotic as Haggis. Coal mining was common in Wales, so some Welsh arrivals knew something about digging a hole and shoring it up to lessen cave ins. The Welsh were known for their singing, not that other people didn't know how to. Like the Scots, most Welsh people were Protestant Christians, a minority being Roman Catholic. Like the others, the Welsh had their own particular accents and in a very diverse way, a penchant for giving places extremely long names which only they can properly pronounce. The Welsh people traditionally love the most noble of the onion family, the leek, making it the floral emblem of Wales.

The English themselves had seen the brunt of many invasions over many centuries. This, of course, led to the development of the English language, the most commonly spoken language on earth, either as a first, second or third language to some. Each area in England had its own accents and customs, a testament to much earlier eras in the historical timeline. It was the English who "united" the United Kingdom, although by mostly using force. By the 1850's, it was the largest empire the world had known, although it had lost the American colonies just seventy years before. It would be the English (British) laws, traditions and institutions that would be firmly implanted on young Sandhurst, the official name of Bendigo until 1891.

There were many other European nationalities represented in this new, burgeoning urban centre, so we will have a look at some of those and what had occurred in Europe prior to the 1850's Eldorado, to quote a Spanish term.

In 1848, most European nations and states experienced domestic, political and social upheavals. Many of these upheavals were outright revolutions. Old monarchies clung to power as the Industrial Revolution transformed lives, although not necessarily for the better. A pamphlet entitled "The Communist Manifesto" would appear at this time and its philosophy would have far reaching impact. The United Kingdom would avoid revolution, although the democratic Chartist Movement and its People's Charter would influence the emerging "new" societies on the Victorian goldfields.

Although the revolutions shook the foundations of the old order in Europe, they were ruthlessly put down. A wave of political exiles fled to avoid severe persecution. Some found their way to Bendigo Creek.

If you were to wander down to the Dick Turner Reserve in Golden Square, you would find the official plaque dedicated to the "Officers and Men of the 1848 Hungarian Revolution". Looked upon as mutineers in the days of the Austro-Hungarian Empire, these men sought sanctuary first in England, then tried to better their situation on the Californian Goldfields in

1849. The plaque commemorates their part in the turbulent year of 1848, as well as indicating that they lived and prospected for gold in that particular vicinity.

ON THIS SITE

HUNGARIAN
OFFICERS AND SOLDIERS
SOUGHT THEIR LUCK AS
GOLD MINERS
AFTER THE SUPPRESSION OF THE

1848
HUNGARIAN REVOLUTION

IN MEMORIAM
THE MELBOURNE HUNGARIAN
COMMUNITY CENTRE
AND
THE HUNGARIAN MINISTRY OF
FOREIGN AFFAIRS

DR. ISTVÁN GYÜRK
AMBASSADOR OF THE REPUBLIC OF HUNGARY

Hungarian Miners Were Here

The fact that large numbers of Germans arrived in this area cannot be disputed – in the 1850's German was regarded as the most common spoken language in Bendigo after English itself. It should be noted that Germany did not exist as a Federation until the 1870's. In the 1850's Germany was a number of Principalities, with a number of cultural differences between them. The Bavarians were renown for the shorts they wore, the Prussians for their military prowess. Interesting to know that in 21st first century Prussia is now part of Poland. The earliest Germans on the goldfields made their way from South Australia, already having laid the foundations for the Barossa Valley wine making industry.

Many French and Swiss immigrants would arrive and stake their tents in Bendigo too. Some had been participants in the 1848 upheavals, many others succumbing to the allure of gold and perhaps "instant" riches. Switzerland is an interesting case when it comes to national identity and language.

The Alpine state can boast three language groups -French, German and Italian.

Speaking of the Italians, many would find their way south: a community of miners digging shallow claims in the Whipstick. The less prosperous Italian miners would build rough shelters from hessian bags, giving one of their number the title of "Mayor of Bagtown". Alberto Maggetti, one of the earlier Whipstick Italian miners, would establish his Wine Hall in Epsom West. This wine hall (also known as the Wallace Reef Wine Hall) would become a favourite spot for the local Italian community, in many ways a cultural community centre. Although Maggetti was also a gold byer, he provided an area for the playing of Italian bowls, which is called Bocce (pronounced bock chay). In the winter the house specially was hot spiced wine. I would not have been surprised if pasta was also prepared in the kitchen. Estimates put the Italians at only around 1% of the population of the time, but at least they could enjoy a little slice of Italia in amongst the wattles and the gums. De-commissioned in the 1930's, it is unfortunate that this legacy of La Dolce Vita was demolished in 1947.

The large German population fanned out across the goldfields, although concentrating in areas such as the Ironbark Gully and German Gully in the Diamond Hill area. Some would go on to establish hotels and a local wine industry. Their attempts to preserve culture would see the establishment of a German speaking school and library – now the Violet Street Primary School in Golden Square.

Many Americans also made the trip to the Bendigo goldfields. Some had been in California during the rushes in 1849, heading to Victoria a few years later as those fields of gold waned. With a strong, independent streak, the Americans would gather at American Flat, American Gully, Californian Gully and California Hill. Just like at Ballarat, the Americans had a reputation for being very well armed, something that would cause Government authorities some concern. Being just 70 years since the American Colonists had succeeded in gaining independence from Britain, they were viewed with official suspicion. On the other hand, the Americans were exemplary in courtesy, especially to women. Some of the Americans were Afro-Americans, usually referred to as "Negros". Small in numbers these descendants of African slaves were shunned most of the time.

There would be several other nationalities to add their voices to the shouts and chatter of this multicultural mix. It is known that there were Polish, New Zealanders (including a few Maoris) Malays, Indians, Dutch, Spanish and even Chileans. The Chilean miners are an interesting example. Making their way from South America to the Californian goldfields, they faced increasing persecution from American miners. With the news of the gold discovery in Victoria, some left a fearful future in California and walked the tracks to Bendigo and Ballarat. Whether they stayed here permanently or made their way back to Chile is unknown. At the very least, they had no need to fear persecution again.

By the mid 1850', as the rush started to slow, the new township of Bendigo (Sandhurst) sported flags of many nations. Many languages could be heard, songs and stories swapped over a campfire and a mug of brew. What formed a union between these men and women had been the lust for gold and an agitation for freedom – highlighted by the unfair and financially difficult gold licence fee. This culminated in the Red Ribbon Movement (or Agitation) in August 1853, when any cultural differences were put aside in pursuit of the common good. When the miners "of all nations" marched to the Government camp at Camp Hill offering a reduced fee for the September licence, they were one people, one cause. The leaders were predominately Scottish Chartists and other intellectuals – they could present an articulate, reasoned submission. At the "Hospital Hill" (around All Saints Church), it was noted that some French and Swiss orators gave fiery speeches to the crowd.

This scenario would be played out on every goldfield until the culmination of the tragic circumstances at Eureka in Ballarat. The people won their freedom, something they didn't have back home. Although I add this as a bit of tongue in cheek, they had demonstrated that the people united will never be defeated. Despite the many cultural differences, they had stood as one people against tyranny and had won.

Those differences were immense, especially given the rapidity of this population explosion. Most of the continental Europeans were Catholic, although many Germans were Lutheran, one of the earliest Protestant Churches. Most of the British people were Protestants, although made up from a number of variant forms. Most Irish were Catholic, although not exclusively. Some wanted an Irish Republic. Just about all of the European nations had been at war with each other over the centuries, empire against empire. Then there were the Jewish people, mostly from Britain, France and Germany. The difference in language, food, customs and history were massive, yet a largely cohesive society began to emerge. This was an enormous "experiment" in diverse people coming together to live together in peace, at least most of the time.

If the reader should think that I've left out a major population group, just keep turning the page. Although there was a very small population prior to 1854, what would eventuate would have ramifications that still haunt some of us well into the 21st century.

CHAPTER FOUR

THE DRAGON'S BREATH

The spirit or ethos that emerged from the heady days of gold and resultant agitation was that this was a new European society being created in a new land. Things would be done differently, for the good of the people. Certainly, the right to vote would be extended to all men, regardless of ownership of property, with the autocratic powers of the Governors broken for all time. Women would still be denied the right to vote and First Nation people were regarded as part of the flora and fauna of the country and treated as such. From the Autumn of 1854, a new agitation would arise on the goldfields that had nothing to do with what would later be termed as "a fair go" – that was an agitation levelled at the Chinese, the echoes of which can still be heard today.

The Chinese miners began arriving in the typical warm and dry Bendigo autumn. Unlike the Europeans, who came out individually or in small groups of friends and family, the Chinese arrived in parties organised along clan lines, headed by an overseer or leader appointed by the clan. The Chinese were from provinces around Canton (Guangdong) and were indentured la-bourers, their fares and provisions paid by the clans. They did so to improve the lives of their impoverished families back home, after repaying the debt to the Chinese clans. The religions of these men were a mixture of Buddhist, Confucian, and Taoist philosophies. They wore long plaited pigtails (queues) at the back of their heads, something quite foreign to the Europeans. The simple shirts and not overly long trousers added to the picture of exotic difference. And they kept coming in increasing numbers.

To the Europeans, the Chinese posed a grave threat to life as they knew it. Stereotypical images were not challenged. The Chinese were regarded as an embodiment of evil – dishonest, opium smoking, non-alcohol drinking, dirty, low moral corrupters of white women and heathens to boot. And we better not forget the Chinese gambling game of Fan Tan. Firstly, the Chinese were regulated by the "headman", who kept a close watch on the behaviour of all in his charge – honesty and lawful behaviour being paramount. Although some of the Chinese were addicted to opium (and opium smoking would flourish in Bendigo and elsewhere), the Europeans obviously had forgotten or didn't know that opium had been introduced into China from India by the British. Just a decade earlier, the Opium Wars lost by China to Britain had been an attempt to stem the supply of the narcotic. The Chinese did drink alcohol, although the amount consumed by the miners was regulated by the leader. Many Europeans drank excessively with resulting undesirable effects. Mining was a dirty business and the Chinese liked a good wash like anyone else. European men frequented the burgeoning brothel trade, usually staffed by white women who had no other means of support. As for the heathen part, well, all I can say is each to their own.

Christianity was seen as the only true religion with all others being irrelevant.

Many Chinese seaports were directly controlled by European powers as well at the United States and Japan – the Chinese Imperial Government being weak, with real power held by the "warlords" throughout the country. It's also fair to say that gambling was not a vice limited to the Chinese – many European miners gambled on a game of cards and the Epsom racecourse was established for a reason.

In the book "History of Bendigo" by George Mackay, it states that a census was taken in April of 1854. At the beginning of that year it was reported that a substantial number of miners had left for other, newer, fields. The population was put at 15,400 persons, with 4,000 being Chinese. It was understood by the non-Chinese inhabitants that this was a British colony, that the white race was supreme amongst all other and the "inscrutable" Chinese were a threat to Christian Civilization and were not welcome.

In June of 1854, Scotsman William Denovan addressed a meeting of around 1.000 miners, calling for a forcible expulsion of the Chinese on July the 4th – American Independence Day. On the eve of the intended expulsion, Denovan was called to the Government camp by Police Magistrate Lachlan McLachlan, also a Scotsman. McLachlan may not have liked the Chinese either, but as part of the official apparatus of Government, he had to enforce strict order on the goldfields. Denovan did what would be called today a "backflip", denying his intention. No such attempt at expelling the Chinese physically took place in Bendigo, although two weeks later another protest meeting against the Chinese was held, with Denovan voicing concerns at the influx of Chinese and calling on government control of Chinese immigration.

The Chinese did face violent opposition in Victoria and the other colonies in the 1850's and 1860's, sometimes on a large scale, sometimes individually. To give you an idea of the prevailing attitudes and methods of the times, via a very young Bendigo Advertiser, we take a short trip up to the north east, the area of the Buckland River goldfield.

Before the days of the "Electric Telegraph", news travelled very slowly across the colony. These events were covered in the Advertiser on Monday, 13th of July 1857. On the 4th of July, a meeting of miners at the Buckland Hotel decided to run the Chinese off that goldfield. Being American Independence Day, the push was led by American miners, no doubt after some "liquid refreshment". The miners chased the Chinese out of their camps, burning tents and other possessions. They were armed with sicks and used them frequently. Police were called in to quell the rioters and many of the Chinese simply would not return to the Buckland. The Advertiser seemed to lovingly support the action – "Pursuing the miserable Mongolians down the river...(the Chinese) evinced their manhood by fleeing before 200 or 300 hundred angry members of the Anglo-Saxon race".

In July of 1861, the savage attack on the Chinese at Lambing Flat – now Young, New South Wales – was reported but this time bravo for the Anglo-Saxon race was missing from the report. There were deaths and horrific injuries inflicted on the otherwise law-abiding Chinese. When the ring leaders of the attacks were rounded-up, the miners burnt down the Police Camp and Courthouse. For some weeks later, the Advertiser would note, "Lambing Flat – all quiet". The spark of the incredibly violent episode was the news from Sydney that the upper house of the New South Wales Parliament had rejected legislation to ban Chinese immigration. I invite you, if you wish, to read the detailed reports of the violence at Lambing Flat in the Advertiser Trove – the National Library of Australia's digitalized newspaper collection. The miners involved were the epitome of what they accused the Chinese to be.

Back to 1855, the Victoria Colonial Government, which consisted of the Governor, Sir Charles Hotham, and the Legislative Council, dominated by squatter and merchant members, brought in a tax of 10 pounds per China-man entering the colony. Just as the First Nation people had been assigned Protectors, the Government assigned Protectors of the Chinese to the gold-field communities, along with interpreters. In 1858, the Government would scrap this tax in favour of an annual residence tax of four pounds. These taxes only applied to the Chinese. The Chinese took the residence tax grimly, organising peaceful protests against them, but to no avail. In a strange turn of events, that wily Scot, William Denovan, supported the Chinese in their objection.

The Chinese, like other miners, were following the golden dream. Some would stay on in Bendigo, some would chase their Dai Gum San (Big Gold Mountain) throughout the continent. The introduction of the original 10 pound tax forced the Chinese making for the Victorian Goldfields to land at Robe in South Australia, making the arduous trek in all seasons. Some never made it to their intended destinations, never to realise the golden dream. All this would set the scene for generations to come – Bendigo and the rest of the country were white, Christian, imperial and "bloody-well proud of it".

CHAPTER FIVE

LITTLE EUROPE

The predominantly European arrivals in Bendigo during the 1850's could be forgiven for wanting to create a slice of Europe down under. Like any other culture or groupings of culture, they knew no other way. That many things were different didn't sway them from their course, with some unpleasant consequences indeed.

Many are the times I have wondered about the cultural shock the local environment meted out to the new arrivals. For example, European summers can be quite warm, but the landscape is a lush green, with plentiful rivers and streams meandering through cities, towns and countryside alike. Winters very cold, quite often accompanied by snow. In this part of the world, summers are usually hot and dry, with dried grass and leaves crunching underfoot. Winters can be frosty, but the cooler weather and rain brings with it a flush of greenery, as Natures revives from the harsh summer sun. The deciduous trees and other plants of Europe were missing, so no displays of Autumn's glowing colours. And let's not forget snakes, tales of which permeated the consciousness and still resounds with us today. There would be another menace that would greet the new arrivals unused to such a threat – the bushfire. Still, they persevered and began creating a planned European style town, as the tents and huts slowly gave way to larger, more permanent structures.

As an integral part of culture, people brought and wore the clothing that they were used to. The clothing represented not only the climatic requirements of Europe, but the strict social mores of the day. In hindsight, which may be a very precious thing, men may have fared a lot better than women. Some wonderful pictures of miners at Chewton in 1858 gives us an idea of the "work garb" of the time. Hats were obligatory at the time, usually with a reasonably sized brim, flat top, often with a colourful band. Shirts were "collarless", sometimes pulled together with a neckerchief (look it up in the dictionary folks!) and usually pocketless. Trousers haven't changed much since them, although the fly sported buttons until zippers were invented. Vests, also known as waistcoats, were popular. Boots completed the miner's attire. It certainly wasn't uncommon for men to be clean shaven, although moustaches or beards were very common. More formal attire included coats, bow ties and shoes. Top hats seemed to be the realm of the more wealthy or self-important.

The ladies of the day were virtually imprisoned in the clothing set by the social standards of the day. Massive "hoop" dresses fanned out from the waist, with multiple petticoat layers underneath. A woman's legs would be completely covered to the foot, then encased by the shoe. It was deemed indecent for a lady to display a bare ankle or two. Long sleeves, never to be rolled up as men could do, gathered at the wrist. It was appropriate for a woman to wear a hat, although bonnets or a lace covering were popular. Colourful, the clothing of the goldfields ladies was more suited to winter than summer, but such was the rigid standard of the day. Children wore pint-sized versions of the above. Much would change over a century and a bit.

The first urban plan for the Bendigo area was drawn up by Captain John Urquhart in 1852. Urquhart had drawn up township provisions at Ravenswood, Bullock Creek and "Happy Jack" (Lockwood), as these had been scenes where early settlements had begun. Urquhart also surveyed a township called "Ballaarat" in 1851 – his original peg is still evident in Sturt Street. Unfortunately for Urquhart's vision, mining and settlement had exploded down the Bendigo Valley and Bendigo Flat. A public meeting in 1853 called on the colonial Government to bring some planning order to the missmash of roads and built structures. Englishman Richard Larritt drew the layout for the new settlement in 1854, thus creating the backbone of streets that still bear fruit in the 21st century.

With planned streets came street planting of more familiar trees. Familiar to Europeans, that is. With the end of the Gold Commission, the former government camp was given over to the new Sandhurst Municipal Council, who decided to establish Rosalind Park in fine European style. The name Rosalind was selected from a character in William Shakespeare's play "As You Like It". Both Charing Cross and Pall Mall were named after famous London thoroughfares. As land was sold, more substantial buildings were erected, both commercial and residential. Styles of buildings would change over time, usually following European trends. It was common for residents to plant gardens of ornamental varieties with abundant vegetable varieties as well.

One of the most influential and revered architects was Carl Wilhelm Vahland, a rather unsuccessful prospector who turned to his original occupation to support himself. It is interesting to note that Vahland would become a British subject, anglicizing his name to William Carl Vahland and joining the Church of England, also known as the Anglican Church. Born before the federation of the German states, Vahland would always refer to himself as being "Hanoverian", or a person from the city of Hanover. With partner Jacob Getzschmann, over 100 buildings would be designed from 1860. Along with other architects, Bendigo was constructed along grand European lines. Looking down Pall Mall from the Alexandra Fountain, one sees a panorama that is typical of any European city.

The earlier Europeans who wished to observe religious rites and holy days either had to do so in groups of their own religious kindred, or on their own. A local Wesleyan preacher, Cornishman James Jeffery, gave a fiery "service" on the general topic of sin early in 1852. A few months later, Dr George Henry Backhaus would establish a Roman Catholic presence on Bendigo Flat. Originally form the German state of Prussia, Backhaus would eventually erect a tent-chapel on Consecrated Flat, the site of St Killian's Church. The Congregationalist Church, Anglican Church, Presbyterian Church and a variety of Methodist Churches would soon be established to meet the religious needs of a multi-religious population. Many variants of Methodists were represented here – Wesleyan, Bible Christians, Primitive, United and Free Methodists. The fact that there were many Protestant Churches, especially under the umbrella name of Methodist, was due to the issue of free will. Unlike Roman Catholics, who largely followed the theology built up over centuries by various Popes, Protestants relied upon adherence to Free Will – which included the free will to interpret Biblical Scripture in various ways. The formation of new Christian churches had never been easy – the Methodists began in the 1700's but were not officially recognised until the 1830's. That the religious differences at time were extreme will be covered in the next chapter.

Religion was seen by the Government as a civilising factor on the goldfields. Certainly robberies, violence and drunkenness were commonplace. The Christian ethos of the day was certainly focused on sin, with hellfire awaiting those who did not repent. The proliferation of alcohol gave rise to another religious movement prevalent throughout Europe and North America, the Temperance Movement which were societies and associations determined to banish alcohol everywhere. Bendigo saw the first Abstinence Society formed in 1857. Unfortunately, not every sinner wished to be saved, especially by force!

As the Churches grew, people had a place to go for regular services and to observe special holy days like Christmas. Even at Christmas, apart from the obvious observance of the birth of Jesus Christ, there was a variety of Christmas traditions also celebrated. To the British, Father Christmas would bring gifts, a rather slender, bearded gentleman in a long green coat. The Germans would celebrate Santa Klaus, the Dutch the black skinned St Nicholas. The Italians would differ substantially with the very feminine Santa Lucia. Naturally European Christmases would fall in the winter, cold with perhaps snow capped everything. The southern Christmas season was typically the opposite; warm to hot, yet the old traditions held fast. It is still something that we "grapple with" today – Christmas cards depicting snow-covered houses, roaring fires, mistletoe and holly, and roast lunches and dinners on days that could fry an egg on concrete.

Despite the entrenchment of Christianity in Bendigo, both the Jewish and Chinese residents of the municipality were able to freely practise their faiths and as such build their own places of worship.

Interestingly those of a non-British background established outlets supporting their cultural preferences. For many years, German butcher shops would provide a variety of meat products based upon the German love of pork. German viticulturalists would bring the first wave of local wine manufacture. Two Danish brothers named Cohn would establish a brewery which would also produce non-alcoholic beverages such as lemonade and cordials. Cohn's products would be sold well beyond the regional boundaries of Bendigo.

The Chinese established various shops, laundries and market gardens. It was in the later that the Chinese would excel well beyond their European counterparts. European customs regarding the watering of plants dictated watering only in the cool of the morning or evening. To do so in the middle of the day was (and still is) considered possibly lethal to the plants. The Chinese would water in the morning, the middle and evenings of the day – no doubt to the relief of the plants sweltering and dehydrating in the heat of a Bendigo summer. Market gardens would be situated around Bendigo, perhaps the most well-known now being the site of Pepper Green Farm, in Thunder Street, very close to the Chinese Joss House. Incidentally, the word "Joss" is derived from the Portuguese word for god, a legacy of the scramble for empire which included Portugal. Much to the angst of non-Chinese residents, the Chinese would establish opium "dens" and gambling houses. That the smoking of opium, or anything else for that matter, was not a good thing, it is here that we find possible tunnel vision when it comes to cultural diversity. The opium smoker would inhale and then need to lie down. The smoker would have the pipe recharged as necessary, spending perhaps many hours in a horizontal position. On the other hand, the European love of alcohol can, in some people, led to fights and even death – accidently or by deliberate intent. Although opium would be made illegal from 1911, alcohol would continue to be sold as a legal, taxed product, much to the chagrin of the growing Temperance Societies who championed the prohibition of alcohol.

Bendigo Joss House

The Chinese were largely shunned by the other residents of Bendigo. Everything about them was regarded with a fearful suspicion. That most were productive, law-abiding members of the overall community seems to have been overlooked. The only time the Chinese would seemingly be made somewhat welcome would be during the Bendigo Easter Fair. There will be more about that later.

People of various national/cultural backgrounds established their own societies and associations as a way of keeping their cultural bonds alive and meaningful. Bendigo was a part of the British Empire after all. Amongst the earliest were the German Deutsche Verein Society, the Scottish Calendonian Society and the Irish Hibernian Society. The Bendigo Advertiser was not always happy with these developments, as it was staunch in its opposition to sectarianism, which it saw as being cultural as well as religious.

Perhaps one of the most unusual cultural observances to be given Public Holiday status in the colony of Victoria was the very Irish St Patricks' Day. St Patrick is the patron saint of Ireland, even though he was a Welsh born Roman citizen. This was the work of Irish born parliamentarian, John O'Shanassey. The Irish population of Bendigo would celebrate this national day held on 17th of March years before it became an official holiday in 1863.

The Advertiser noted, rather whimsically, on the 18th of March 1856 that: "Yesterday, being the day devoted to the honour of Ireland's patron saint, was honoured by the closing of the banks. It is hoped that the police-sheet of today will not contain the names of the very many who were locked up for the innocent offence of 'wetting their shamrock'". On the occasion of it becoming an official holiday for all in 1863, a Ball and Supper was held at the premises of Reynolds and English, on the corner of Hargreaves and William-son Streets. The Advertiser recorded the details of the grand event, noting that the Reverend Backhaus caused a minor upset when he said something to a group of attendees who took great offence. What was said was not published. The incident was quickly resolved as being due to a misunder-standing of what the Prussian born priest had actually said. I think we can assume at this point that there may have been a minor clash of cultures, especially if those offended had been 'wetting their shamrock'.

This public holiday would last well into the twentieth century, when simply it could no longer be justified, especially with the development of other special days. Over the decades, there would be the St Patrick's Day Parade in the central business district, horse racing and other sporting events, a range of Irish musical and poetic recitals – all things Irish. Indeed, it became a day when non Irish people could become "Irish", usually washed down with various quantities of beers and/or whisky. I should point out that not everyone was overly pleased with this celebration dedicated to a Roman Catholic saint.

The great British invention – the railway – would link Bendigo and Mel-bourne together in 1862. No longer did travellers need to take the arduous, long and risky trip by foot, horse or by coach. Deep quartz mining was un-derway, with commerce, trade and industries booming. Theatres did a roar-ing trade; sporting clubs were established – all the hallmarks of a successful and prosperous European city. Various charitable funds would try to help the poor and Bendigo even sported its own Volunteer Rifle Corps and Volun-teer Cavalry Regiment for the defence of Queen and Empire. For the Dja Dja Wurrung people still in the area, it must have been a bewildering sight.

But all that glitters is not gold, for many who came to build little Europe did not leave the worst of old Europe behind. In what was a new European society, the chance to create something incredibly and powerfully new was fractured by old hatred, intolerance and an inability to truly "live and let live" – most of it being founded on the idea that there is only one God – MY GOD!

CHAPTER SIX

MINE IS BETTER THAN YOURS

Religion can be a double-edge sword. Over the ages, it has given multitudes of people a framework to structure their lives around, giving comfort, strength and hope. It has also been able to bridge cultural diversity between people of various languages, cultures and ethnicity. However, religion has been a cause of much conflict, tyranny and persecution, involving countless millions of people. When we talk of sectarianism, we are talking about bigotry between members of difference religions and bigotry within members of the same overall religious path.

The first sectarian conflict in the Bendigo region was perpetrated by the pastoralists and their employees. The Christian Europeans, with many varying degrees of Christian adherence, disregarded the spiritual traditions of the Dja Dja Wurrung wholesale. The same could be said of the gold seekers with the occupation and desecration of First Nation sacred sites and Country. Religious superiority seemed to go hand in hand with attitudes of racial superiority – superiority of any kind is hard to overcome. Despite some of the new European community wanting to leave sectarianism behind in old Europe, many settlers brought it along like a treasured heirloom they simply wouldn't disregard, even for the better.

The Bendigo Advertiser, established in 1853, was a champion of anti-sectarianism, although it was also a champion of anti-Chinese and other anti "Asiatic" sentiment.

The Victorian Parliament began the long and difficult road to state education as early as 1858, state education finally getting the full green light in 1872. An Advertiser correspondent's viewpoint appeared on Monday, 8 February 1858, in relation to the First Education Bill.

> "I am convinced that the majority of parents are in favour of secular education, combined with religious instruction, but sectarian jealousy and proselytism interpose serious, and, in fact almost insuperable obstacles in the way of its adoption."

Incidentally, proselytism means to convert people to one's own faith or cause. The following month, a new government formed by the very Irish John O'Shanassey and Deputy Charles Gavan Duffy alarmed Protestants throughout the colony. Both wanted an Irish Republic and were Catholic – Duffy had produced a newspaper in Ireland at the time of the 1848-49 Troubles and had been arrested for sedition. The Editorial in the Advertiser on Wednesday 23rd June 1858 gives an idea of rising tension in Bendigo and the Colony itself. The editorial was headed: "The Bondage of Bigotry".

> "We do not like the symptoms which have manifested themselves of late of the growth of the spirit of sectarianism, and of religious jealousies in this colony...may Heaven especially save people of this colony from falling into that of the bondage of Bigotry".

The majority of Irish were Catholic, many with strong anti-English/republican sentiments. The smaller population of Northern Irish were mostly protestant (Church of Ireland and Presbyterian), and were fiercely loyal to the Crown. Catholics and Protestants generally had a dislike or a strong opposition to each other. Inter marriage between Catholics and Protestants could be compared to European women marrying Chinese men. This intolerance would last well into the twentieth century, until Christian Churches began to close from dwindling attendances.

When the local Protector of the Chinese, Mr Standish, was appointed Commissioner of Police by John O'Shanassey in August 1858, there was a hue and cry from Protestants – Standish was Catholic and the appointment fuelled fears that Catholics were somehow on the rise. In the editorial of

Tuesday 17th of August 1858, the Advertiser excelled in a poetic response worthy of William Shakespeare:

> "Whatever the religious belief of the Chinese Protector, it must be admitted that he made no special display of it, and that he could scarcely be taken for a zealot in sectarian matters. Of all men to fix upon him as a candidate likely to inspire sectarian-religious predilections, is as precious a piece of humbug as any scandal mongering noodle ever made himself ridiculous by".

The Advertiser could both be supportive and critical of both Catholics and Protestants, depending on the issue at hand. When the Scots of Bendigo founded the Bendigo Caledonian Society in February 1859, the Advertiser was quite critical of this development. From the Editorial of the 15th of February, the Advertiser did say that it was supportive of people honouring "their love of home and pride of country" and was supportive of the Society in "raising a fund which may be available for the relief of necessities of their distressed countrymen". However, in a tone of grave concern, it continued: "Is not such a movement calculated to divide them from their fellow colonists and split the community into national factions?". The Advertiser hoped that the Caledonian Society "wouldn't become a political one, or tend to develop dissentions of which rather too evident symptoms have already been manifest in this district, as well as in other parts of the colony". In a call to what we can term the Culture of Empire, the newspaper ended with "But Britons in a British community should be united...". The next day, a letter by Scotsman William Denovan gently repudiated the Editorial concern: "the Bendigo Caledonian Society is purely a social institution, and nothing more". I speculate that by 1859, the mysterious Haggis had made its first triumphant appearance in the Bendigo valley.

Although I feel it is highly likely that some residents did put religious differences aside, (after all, it was and is a personal choice) "battle lines" were drawn as Catholic and Protestant action groups were formed, some far more militant than others. Even the Temperance Movement was split on sectarian lines – there was the Catholic Temperance Society, with the Protestants building the Temperance Hall in View Street. At the time of writing, the Hall is occupied by a dance school, complete with leotards. The puritanical members of the hall would be groaning in shocked disbelief if they knew!

The establishment of the Orange Lodges (which paid homage to the victory of William of Orange over Catholic James II of England at the battle of the Boyne in 1690) saw a more militant, anti-Catholic voice appear throughout the colony. Likewise, Hibernian (Irish) Societies and local St Patrick's Day committees would see a more militant anti-Protestant/English voice arise. These were the "Green" organisations of their days – Orange representing Protestantism, Green representing Catholicism, although with a strongly southern Irish bent. This polarisation would occur throughout the continent, only abating in the 1970's.

So why would some Protestants be vehement towards Catholics and their church and establish groups to 'defend' against them? After all, they were Christians. The answer, in summary, goes back to the Reformation, or split in the then single Christian Church (even though there already existed Coptic and Orthodox Christianity). The Catholic Church's attempt to stamp out what were seen as heretics, or traitors, to the true faith were both vicious and unrelenting. Torture and execution of those now opposed to the Church of Rome ranged across central and western Europe, as well as central and southern America. To be fair, Oliver Cromwell, during the English Civil War, ordered brutalities against English people who would not renounce the Pope and Papal authority. The Orangemen were fierce defenders of "individual responsibility and right of private judgement" and were opposed to the Catholic Church's "domination" over people's lives. It was noted as well that Protestant nations showed great industrial prosperity over Catholic nations, all explained by greater personal free will. On the other hand, the Catholic Church of the day had seen the Reformation as a rebellion against the "True" Church – according to the story, the Apostle Peter had been selected by Jesus to be "the rock upon which I shall build my church". Peter allegedly went to Rome, ending his days with crucifixion by the Romans, although upside-down according to the legend. Orange Lodges were established throughout the British Empire, as well an in predominantly Catholic France, Italy and Spain.

The Orange Lodges celebrated the victorious Battle of the Boyne on the 12th of July every year. It was, to them, as much a glorious day as St Patrick's Day was to the Irish – especially Irish Catholics. The odd thing about it was the choice of date – the Battle of the Boyne actually occurred on the 10th of July 1690. In 1861, the threat of a very real, violent clash between the two bickering Christian perspectives seemed inevitable, right here in Bendigo. I will summarise what occurred from a lengthy article from the Advertiser of Saturday 12th July 1861. The article is headed: "Threatened Riot". The previous day some informants had come to the Police Camp stating that numerous Irish Orangemen were going to celebrate with an Orange Ball and Supper at the Catherine Reef Hotel, Peg Leg, and then march in procession into Sandhurst, as Bendigo was officially known. The informants continued that a large number of armed, Irish Catholic men were coming from Huntly, Epsom, Bendigo Flat and other places, to prevent the Orangemen from entering the centre of town. On hearing this information, the Municipal Police Force was mobilised by Magistrate McLachlan and the Municipal Chairman (Mayor) Mr J.J.Casey. At around 3 o'clock in the afternoon, intelligence was received that about 100 persons were seen proceeding along the Eaglehawk Road, although quietly enough, in the direction of the Catherine Reef Hotel. The Police, who were mounted, took off towards Eaglehawk. By the time they arrived, Sergeant Richards had instructed the Orangemen that there was to be no Ball, no supper and no demonstration of any kind whatsoever. Although thoroughly disappointed, the Orangemen quietly dispersed. It was noted that the hotel was still preparing for the event, but Mr McLachlan and Mr Casey ordered the hotel closed and an Orange flag taken down. The publican, Mr Ellis had to oblige, even though permission for the Orange event had been sought from, and grated by Mr Mollison J.P. Incidentally, the flying of the Orange flag in Victoria had been outlawed by an Act of Parliament instigated by the very Irish John O'Shanassey! The Advertiser commended the actions of the authorities, by the way. As our dear local rag continued, the large number of armed Green would-be combatants never materialised. Speculating that the threatened riot may have been just a rumour, methinks to sabotage the Orangemen, the Advertiser roared against anyone who thought that taking up arms against others was justified, and hoped "that an example will be made of any such offenders that can be found".

Violent clashes between the Orange and the Green were quite common, especially in Ireland and elsewhere. In 1870-71, riots in New York would see over 70 dead with many more injured. We were spared the vilest of religious intolerance between and within the Christian traditions.

As a footnote, the Ulster Loyal Orange Lodge of Bendigo went to the Camp Hotel instead. Dancing to midnight, they quietly proceeded to the Catherine Reef Hotel for supper until daylight. This was the third annual celebration of the Battle of the Boyne in Bendigo. In a letter to the Editor, from the 16th of July 1861, William Cuthbert, member of the lodge, stated that no yellow or orange flag was on display, so could not have been taken down by order. He claimed that "the society have not nor ever had one" and displaying such a flag would be in breach of the Act, and "...Orangemen have generally been known as law upholders and not law breakers. Besides, it might have hurt the feelings of many of our fellow countrymen." Cuthbert did state that the Union Jack flag was displayed outside the hotel, with the English Ensign and French Tri-Colour displayed within.

The very first official, and widespread. St Patrick's Day in 1983 did not go ahead without some disruptive behaviour. The day before, the 16th of March 1863, the Advertiser proclaimed in its editorial that:

> "Neither Limerick nor Derry has anything to do with the natal day of the benevolent, though somewhat apocryphal old saint. Serenely, he may look down upon both green and orange flags...It is the fusion of race, and class, and sect which will make Victoria a great nation".

Two days later, when reporting the Ball and supper, mention was made of several persons trying to disrupt the celebrations. Seriously outnumbered, and with possible police intervention, the disrupters simply gave up and dispersed. Given that no further details were given, we can only speculate the not everyone in Bendigo was pleased with this new public holiday. It should be noted the Calendonian Society (and other groups), fully supported St Patrick's Day. On the other hand, the St Patrick's Day Committee would continually refuse to allow the Orange Lodges to participate in the annual St Patrick's Day processions.

Before we leave Sectarianism in the nineteenth century (where it should have stayed!), I would be remiss not to mention a very special day/night that was part of British culture and celebrated annually in Bendigo until the 1980's. That day/night was the 5th of November – Guy Fawkes night, usually referred to as 'cracker night".

In the year 1605, a group of militant Catholics devised a plan to blow up the Houses of Parliament, while the Protestant King James 1 was present. The conspirators hoped to replace the assassinated James with a Catholic monarch. As odd as it seems to us today, the conspirators rented a building across the road from Parliament, a passageway connecting the building to a cellar under the Parliament Houses. The cellar was loaded up with kegs of gunpowder, with Guy Fawkes being given the duty of lighting the slow burning fuses on the 5th of November. As Fawkes entered the cellar via the passageway, he was arrested by soldiers – an anonymous letter to the Catholic Lord Monteagle had warned him to stay away as something was afoot. Rising above religious difference, Lord Monteagle had altered the authorities.

Ever since that failed plot, throughout England and its growing empire, the "Protestant Victory" was celebrated with bonfires and fireworks. It was an English tradition to make an effigy of Fawkes and toss it onto the bonfire – symbolising being burnt at the stake. Actually, Fawkes was set to be publicly hanged, but as he reached the decking of the rather tall gallows, he slipped and fell breaking his own neck. It is interesting to note, from my own experience, that Catholic families would enjoy cracker night as much as anyone else. Incidentally, Chinese traders did a roaring trade in fireworks given they imported them for their own purposes anyway. Local milk bars and department stores would stock fireworks until they were outlawed some 30 years ago. Apparently, it had something to do with an increasing number of children sustaining injuries. Well I do remember going into Coles, when it was just a department store, coming out with a plastic bag full of assorted explosives. All for one dollar, by the way.

We will revisit Sectarianism in Bendigo as a new century began – truthfully it has caused such widespread and ongoing conflict and misery worldwide. Although Bendigo, like most of colonial Victoria, was quite a multicultural society, the Culture of Empire was paramount. The British Empire was at its peak – therefore all things British were officially regarded as the zenith of all civilization. Despite this overriding ethos, room was given in the "new country" to others from other lands to practise their faiths and traditions, something those people could not do if they were still in the British Isles.

CHAPTER SEVEN

OTHER VOICES, OTHER FAITHS

Before we look at the non-Christian members of the earlier Bendigo community, we should mention those smaller Christian groups present. All Protestant, their minority status, as well as their own philosophies at times, would put them on the "outer edges" of Christian faith.

Of these minority Christian faiths, a few originated in the United States. These faiths are still present in Bendigo today. In nineteenth century Bendigo, there were small congregations of Jehovah's Witnesses, Seventh Day Adventists and Mormons, also officially known as the Church of Jesus Christ of Latter Day Saints. This last group was quite distinctive as "The Book of Mormon" is said to be another testament of Jesus Christ, given to the American Joseph Smith via gold tablets in a strange language in 1830's America. The Seventh Day Adventist's were/ are vegetarians and, along with Jehovah Witnesses, held church services on the original Sabbath or Holy Day, which was Saturday.

The Free Masons, made up of and available to all Protestant men, is an ancient society dedicated to service. It was never open to Catholics, however er Jewish men could gain membership, as Freemasonry dates back to the time of Solomon. When the outstanding Masonic Hall was built in View Street, designed by Mason William Vahland, the Orange Lodges would have their Battle of the Boyne observances there. It should be noted that not every Mason was an Orangemen and visa versa. There was also a rise in Spiritualism, which indulged in seances and that sort of thing. William Denovan, originally a Congregationalist Christian, became a Spiritualist in the late 19th century.

Then there were the Chinese, the most numerous of the non-European/Christian population of Bendigo. The Bendigo Advertiser frequently used the term "Chinkers" or "Chinkies" when referring to the Chinese. This gives us an idea of how they were generally referred to a century or more ago, and generally regarded as well. It is now believed that there were as many as twenty Joss Houses in Bendigo, with only two being made of brick – wonderfully, local made Chinese bricks which are thinner than what we are usually accustomed to. Well fired at the Chinese Brick Works in Thunder Street, they were very resilient bricks, often superior to some bricks from other local manufacturers. Some Joss Houses were located on High Street, Golden Square, Williams Road Eaglehawk, the Long Gully Camp and the Ironbark/Emu Point Camp in Finn Street, as well as other locations. The well-known Ironbark Joss House is the only survivor, being constructed from August 1870 to January1871. In that year (1871), Chinese New Year was celebrated soon after, making that occasion even more auspicious. This Joss House followed ancient tradition by being dedicated to the God Kwan Gung. A Chinese General, who lived from 221 to 266 A.D, Kwan Gung was regarded as being forthright, just, as well as making men successful in their ventures and very courageous. This place of worship was probably operated by the See Yap Society, as the Society had its rooms located in the Ironbark Camp.

The Chinese brought their faith and festivals with them. As part of the tradition, ceremonial banners, weapons, costumes and dragons were imported from China. We certainly cannot forget that firecrackers were almost obligatory in every cultural event, whether it be Chinese New Year, Harvest or Spring Festivals or beginning their march to the CBD almost every Easter from 1879. The Chinese loved theatre as much as Europeans, with the first travelling tent theatre being established at the Ironbark Camp in 1859. Chinese operas could go on for a very long time – the Bendigo Advertiser noted in its edition of Tuesday 23rd April 1889: "This opera takes seven years to render in full, but those who patronise it are not compelled to sit it out".

The opera referred to was titled "Lykim No" or "The Shining Sun Shorn of its Shirt". According to the Advertiser, it was written 17 centuries ago.

To most Europeans, the Chinese were something to fear and loath – increasing Chinese migration only served to fuel those fears. Christianity "reigned supreme" in Bendigo, at least from a European perspective, with the Chinese faith being regarded as completely worthless. Some of the most predominant Christian Churches in Bendigo, and elsewhere, took it upon themselves to try and convert the Chinese to the Christian faith, thereby saving them from "the Lake of Eternal Fire", or hell as it is usually known. The Wesleyan Church began its mission at the Ironbark Camp in 1867. The Anglican Church followed suit at the same camp in 1871. And yes, some Chinese did renounce their traditional faith and convert to Christianity. Anglican Chinese converts built a very decorative chair for the Bishop at St Paul's Cathedral.

With very few Chinese women ever making to these shores, it would be inevitable that some Chinese men would partner with European women – much to the disgust of most European residents. The women would be regarded as little more than prostitutes and treated accordingly. Precious little difference was made of those women who had married Christian converted Chinese men. It is interesting to note that some Chinese men adopted European dress and customs as the nineteenth century went along. In a sense it didn't do their popularity much good, as racial fervour against the Chinese and other non-Europeans continued to escalate.

As we have seen, at least the Chinese were given the opportunity to freely practise their faith and their festivals. Certainly, they were not obliged to drop all of that and assimilate to "full" European Culture, ignoring their own heritage. We will keep revisiting the Chinese in Bendigo, as they are a big part of Bendigo's multicultural story since the discovery of gold brought the world to the banks of Bendigo Creek.

If any people on Earth have been the most persecuted and shunned throughout human history, then surely it is the Jewish people, That's not to say that all other people on Earth have held this perspective, likewise, most cultural groups have experienced some persecution at one time or another. Certainly, the pages of history are more than dotted with the persecution of one or more cultures by another. When it comes to the Jewish people – generally regarded as a combination of religion, race and identity – they have suffered bigotry and violence for a long time. Why is this so? From the Christian, European viewpoint, two main reasons emerge. The first is that the Jews were allowed to lend money with interest being paid back to them. In ancient times, the non-Jewish people – collectively known as the Gentiles – could lend money but were forbidden to charge interest on the loans. Henceforth, Jewish people gained the reputation for being greedy. The Gentiles either forgot, (or weren't aware) that in Jewish culture every 50th year was a Jubilee Year, a year when all debt would be erased automatically. The second reason dates from the execution of Jesus, who Christians see as the Son of God. According to New Testament Scripture, the Roman Governor of Jerusalem, Pontius Pilates, gave the Jewish people the opportunity to have Jesus freed, but they declined. (The Gospel of Matthew gives a different account of that occasion than the common views expressed in Mark, Luke and John.) Thereafter, the Jewish people were regarded as having allowed the death of Jesus, the Messiah or Saviour, the actual son of God.

The Jewish Torah forms the basis for the Christian Old Testament in the Bible, while in Islamic tradition it is known as "The Book". In the many centuries before the discovery of gold in the Bendigo Valley, Jewish people had encountered persecution, segregation and even massacres as they settled throughout Europe. It was in Europe that a new form of their original Hebrew language would develop – Yiddish. Notable, some Jewish people did remain in Jerusalem and its region, experiencing a number of invasions and conquests.

Just like many other people from around the world, Jewish gold seekers made their way to Bendigo. The first known Jewish religious service appears to have been held in a tent in 1853, with a Mr Moses and Mr Joseph leading the service. The English, German and Russian Jewish congregation was believed to have numbered a few hundred. It is possible that Jewish miners from other parts of Europe may have been at the services as well. Two years later, regular services were held at the residence of Mr Woolf at Market Square, the current abode of the Bendigo Library.

Not every Christian was ready to employ a Jewish worker, so those Jewish men who had raised some capital from gold established various businesses – one of the best known being the Criterion Hotel on the corner of Mundy and Dowling Streets. Dowling Street would be renamed Hopetoun Street, so I shall use the more modern name unless otherwise indicated.

Like other religious groups, the Jewish people pf Bendigo needed a proper place of worship. The Victorian Government granted the Jewish people land for the purposes of building a Synagogue near the junction of Hopetoun and Mundy streets, but not the actual junction now occupied by a tyre company. This land grant in late 1855 is quite important for a couple of very good reasons. Firstly, British Law prevailed in the colony and that Law did not give full citizenship to Jewish people, even those born in the U.K. It would not be until Lord Lucan's Bill of 1858 that British Jews would receive full status, which included the right to openly practice their faith. In the Victorian Parliament of that same year, Mr John O'Shanassey introduced a similar Bill, which easily passed into law. That would explain why the 1855 grant was not Gazetted officially until 1858 – technically speaking, it was against the law for a Government to give the Jewish people the opportunity to build a proper place of worship. Secondly, the 1855 grant shows that there was a new wind for acceptance blowing through the colony, at least for the freedom of religion. The 1858 law also gave male British subjects who were Jewish the right to vote.

The local Jewish community advertised a tender in November 1855 for the erection of a weatherboard building for their use. By July 1856, the first synagogue in Bendigo was ready to be consecrated. What follows is from a very detailed description of the opening by the Bendigo Advertiser, in its edition of Monday, 14th July 1856. The paper described the new building as being made of wood, lined with cedar on the interior, surrounded by benches, with a "pulpit" where there would be a chorus (singers) and where the teacher would preside. Although the report details that there were about "50-100", there is no mention of a Rabbi. Rather it appears that the Trustees of the Synagogue would conduct the services. Mr Henry Moses gave an address, part of which is detailed here:

"Our native England has been surpassed by her colonies in giving us the same freedom as other religious bodies, we may hope to see that our co-religionists in Europe will receive that freedom, which, as men, as citizens and subjects, they have an imperishable right to"...(the punctuation is the Advertiser's, not mine.) Mr Moses continued:

"to allow no religious prejudices to interfere between us and our deities, to remember that there is but one God, before whom all men are equal, that through we may all have our own particular road to the grand goal..."

What strikes me about this speech is its heartfelt sincerity and thankful-ness at being able to freely practise their faith. These sentiments still echo around the world today, where formerly oppressed people are given the opportunity to have a new life, free from religious intolerance.

The first known "Rabbi" to be appointed to Bendigo was Isaac Friedman in 1858. This leads to an interesting question: Jewish people eat Kosher, or sanctified/blessed meat, so who conducted that particular ritual before that appointment? We can only guess that one or more of the Trustees carried out that function. The 'Reverend' Friedman (as the Advertiser put it) may not have been a fully ordained Rabbi, rather a chazen and schochet to the congregation. These terms apply to someone who leads the people and is certified by a rabbi or Jewish Court to slaughter animals for food according to Jewish Law.

The Bendigo Jewish community was probably the smallest in the colony and, like other people, Jewish people did relocate to other centres depend-ing on their own wishes and requirements. Both Ballarat and Geelong had congregations, as well as Lonsdale and Bourke Streets in Melbourne.

By 1859 though, the Jewish community in Victoria did not seem to be faring all that well. In what was a revolutionary and controversial move, the Victorian Colonial Parliament decided to provide a one-off grant for the re-lief of Jewish congregation. On January 27, 1860, the Treasury issued the following grants:

1,200 Pounds to Bourke Street

300 pounds to Lonsdale Street

250 pounds to Geelong

150 to Ballarat

100 Pounds to Sandhurst (Bendigo)

The Bendigo congregation received the smallest grant, possibly due to its size.

To give you an idea of how people of the day defined Jewish people, I think the following extract from the Advertiser of 1 November 1860 sums it all up. The extract comes from the review of the play "Oliver Twist" which was playing in Bendigo. The reviewer is referring to actor Mr C.W.Barry, who played the role of Fagin – the organiser of a group of child pickpockets:

> "In no one character in which this gentleman has appeared since his arrival here has he displayed the same aptitude for any part as he did for that of the avaricious, grasping Jew".

This Character, Fagin, was modelled on notorious London criminal, Ikey Solomon, who escaped from Newgate Prison to the U.S. via Denmark. When Solomon's wife was deported for criminal offences to Hobart in 1828, he travelled to Hobart and opened a tobacco and general store. He was arrested in 1829 and returned to England. The name Fagin was from a friend of author Charles Dickens, when he was a young factor worker.

Towards the end of September 1862, the Bendigo Jewish Community hosted a special night at the Temperance Hall in View Street, featuring a Rabbi from Jerusalem. Although a theological address was to be given, in Hebrew by the way, it was also meant to raise funds for elderly Jews in Jerusalem. It would also serve as a kind of interfaith gathering, perhaps the first in Bendigo. What follows is a summary from the Advertiser, Monday 29 September 1862.

Rabbi Hyan Zavee Sneersohn was travelling to various parts of the world acting as a fundraising missionary. Bendigo may have only been a decade old, but certainly tales of golden riches had obviously been heard in the ancient city. The Rabbi gave a historical lecture with the impressive title of: "The Restoration of Israel and the Sub-Biblical History of Jerusalem, from the destruction of the second Temple to the present time".

Although presented in Hebrew, the Anglican Minister Reverend Croxton read the English translation. On the "platform" were Reverends Fletcher, Daniel and Nish. The Chairman of the Municipality, Mr Burrowes, presided at the event. After the lecture, Reverends Fletcher, Daniel and Nish, along with William Denovan, gave "moving addresses". A resolution was called and passed for the collection of subscriptions (donations) with a committee to be formed for the purpose – not a small committee by the way. The members were Reverends Croxton, Fletcher, Nish, Daniel and Hart, with Messrs Burrowes, R. Strickland MLA, W.D.C. Denovan, H. Joseph, H. Jackson, G.P. Joseph, L. Myers, B. Joseph, J. Cohn, B. Lazarus, A. Alexander and Mr Samuel.

Then the Letters to the Editor page exploded. It should be noted that back then many authors of such letters could hide behind a "nom de plume" or pen name. On Wednesday 1 October 1862,

Mr "ANTI-HUMBUG" wrote a searing rebuttal of the fund: "... it appears to me, that the time chosen for asserting their rights, viz, begging, is so peculiarly mal-a-propos that I trust you will allow me space for a few words on the subject". Mr AH went on to list a number of appeals then current in Bendigo, or, as he put it, "in the thick of" – Lancashire Relief Fund, the Irish distress, the Refuge for Unfortunate Females, aid to the Church and so forth. He speculated that there would soon be subscriptions to the Races and to the Council "to liquidate their debt". Being critical of the council is obviously not a new thing dear reader! Mr AH ended with "There may be distress, but where is there not, and why not relieve unfortunate countrymen at home before utter strangers". Two things are apparent here – the first being the use of the word "begging" when referring to the Jewish appeal (it does not seem to apply to others) and secondly that charity begins at home ethos, still prevalent today. It is clear that Bendigo residents did donate to a range of appeals, local and abroad.

The next edition saw Mr ANTI-PHARISEE" attacking the Reverend Croxton personally, who was actively seeking donations by door knocking. Although Mr AP stated that it wasn't his intention "to question the propriety of giving distressed Jews relief here or elsewhere", his point was that the Anglican would not personally contribute to Bendigo Hospital, nor would he allow a collection to be made in his church for "our best institution". He ended by writing; "I do not like to attribute motives to any man, but I cannot help thinking that some explanation is required."

The following day, Mr "HUMANITY" wrote a strong objection to Mr "AN-TI HUMBUG's letter stating: "Had he boldly objected on the score of his religious bigotry, I could at least have given him credit for honesty of purpose". We do not know if Mr H was Jewish or Gentile.

They were not the only letters on the subject, just a sample. Despite some conflicting views on the matter, the Advertiser reported on Friday 24 October 1862 that:"...the appeal met with a liberal and charitable response to their call for the immediate relief of the poor Jews in Jerusalem; accompanied, doubtless, by the earnest prayer that the restoration of the Holy Land to the Jews, and their taking up of their abode there for all ages to come, was not far distant". That restoration occurred in 1948 and we all know what happened next...The Jewish population of Bendigo would ebb and flow, and ebb again into the twentieth century. Certainly, some local Jewish people did well out of being in business and holding mining interests. I did see a reference to a German and a Russian Jewish Hawker. Their number as hawkers seems to have been very small indeed, given that other nationalities would represent the majority of the carted-street sellers of various goods.

When Reverend Friedman resigned in 1868, Bendigo Jews were left without an official cleric until the appointment of Isaac Stone in 1870. The original timber synagogue was now 14 years old and it was decided that a newer, far more impressive building would be required – on the same site. In early 1872, the firm of Vahland and Getzschmann had provided an appropriate design to the Jewish community and a rather rapid construction of the new brick synagogue was begun. Although some reports of the cost and capacity of the new synagogue do differ substantially from other reports, it would appear that the ground floor and gallery could seat at least 300 people and cost at least 1,300 pounds to construct. The dimensions of the interior were given as 11 square metres for the ground floor with the ladies' gallery seven metres by six metres in area. The exterior was built and designed in red and white bricks, the height from floor to ceiling given as being just over nine metres, with an octagonal dome of over five metres in height rising from the roof. In total, the height of the new synagogue was given as being 15 metres. On the top of each corner of the synagogue were placed "turrets", each topped by a small dome. The new Bendigo Synagogue was consecrated by "Reverend" Stone on the 29th September 1872. There are reports that it wasn't quite finished, possibly due to financial constraints. This was rectified three years later.

There were some weddings conducted in the new building as well as regular Holy Day services. In 1880, Isidore Myers, from East Melbourne, would be appointed as the new Rabbi for Bendigo upon the end of Isaac Stone's tenure. Although the congregation began to wane from the 1880's, at that time there was a small Jewish school operating with around 50 pupils receiving instruction in Hebrew, grammar, faith and the teaching of the Torah (which are the first five books of the Christian Bible). However, by the end of the 1800's the local Jewish population was in significant decline.

Non-Jewish women who married Jewish men, could not be buried in Jewish sections of local cemeteries when they shuffled off this mortal coil. Often mentioned on their husband's tombstones, the wives would be buried in their respective Christian sections, or perhaps in the unmarked Pauper's section of the cemetery. Even in death, strict protocols had to be observed.

Before we leave this section, I feel it is appropriate to give a summary of the life of Simcha Myer Baevski, otherwise known to us as Sidney Myer.

Born into a Jewish family in modern day Belarus in 1875, Simcha experienced firsthand the poverty of being Jewish in Russia and the violent "pogroms" against them in the old Tsarist state. When Simcha emigrated to Australia in 1899, he was penniless and had to teach himself English. His brother Elcon had arrived two years earlier and they both worked in fabric and clothing stores in Melbourne. In 1900, the brothers opened a small drapery store in Bendigo with Simcha supplementing the demand for fabrics and clothing in country districts, first by foot and later with a horse drawn cart. Their good taste and developing business skills soon enabled them to expand into new premises in Pall Mall. Unfortunately, a rift between the brothers would soon develop over the observance of the Sabbath – no work to be done on Saturdays. Elcon insisted that they could not trade on Saturdays, Simcha insisted that they couldn't miss the most important trading day of the week. The partnership ended, with Elcon returning to Melbourne to begin his own fabrics business, Simcha becoming the sole proprietor of Myer. It should be noted that Elcon would supply his brother's burgeoning business for the rest of his life. Simcha became Sidney Myer and married a Jewish woman in the Ballarat Synagogue in 1905. In 1911, Sidney Myer bought premises in Melbourne's Bourke Street and the rest is retail history.

In 1919, on a trip to Reno, Nevada, in the United States of America, Sidney Myer would divorce his first wife, probably because it was easier to do so there. That divorce was not legally recognised in Australia, nor was his second marriage, in Reno, to a Gentile woman, who was Anglican. That marriage 'conveniently' took place in January 1920, with Sidney Myer renouncing Judaism by becoming Anglican as well. The children of that marriage would all be born in the United States, to give them some sort of legal status. To the Australian authorities, who never recognised the second marriage, those children would have the rather rough status as being "illegitimate", being born outside the law, without any legal rights to inheritance and so forth. In common parlance, such children could legally be called "bastards".

Although we might overlook Sidney Myer's marriages, what we can't overlook is the essence of his story. Seeking a safe haven from violent oppression, the migrant did what it took to create a new life in a new, although transplanted, European society. In a religious minority in a reasonably welcoming Bendigo community, Myer created a retail empire that began in Bendigo. He was able to develop and implement skills that gave employment opportunities to local people, then much further afield. This he simply could not have achieved in Russia. Sidney Myer died in 1931 at the age of 51 and his passing was mourned by tens of thousands of people.

As with the Chinese, we'll leave the Jewish community here, although they will be mentioned again and again in subsequent chapters. The next group, I can assure you dear reader, certainly needs to be mentioned. Although small in number, these people were very solid members of the British Empire and vocally proud of it too. There were only two perceived problems 1) they were not white, and 2) they were not Christian.

When the Advertiser wrote about anyone from India, they were all referred to as being "Hindoo" which was the common European spelling of Hindu. During the research for this book, I became acutely aware that the

Advertiser didn't have a fact checking department anywhere in sight. The spelling of a name for an individual could easily change from one day to another, *and* there could be quite glaring mistakes that missed the Editor's eye. The best example of this come from the Advertiser of Wednesday, 19th April 1899, in a description of a "Hindoo" hawker having eight pounds and 16 shillings stolen from his room at the Bendigo Hotel. A young man was arrested for the crime, with the court proceedings being reported in the press. Throughout the saga, the "Hindoo" hawker's name was given as being Abraham Solomon – far more Jewish than Hindu and probably more European than Indian. Work that one out ladies and gentlemen!

Although there were a number of Europeans who obtained a hawker's license to earn a living, from the 1880's onwards an influx of migrants from India would swell the ranks of the street cart vendors in Bendigo and elsewhere. Being part of the British Empire, all Indians were British subjects, with men having the automatic right to vote in colonial parliamentary elections before any woman could. My research indicated that there were few actual Hindus residing in Bendigo, although the hawking population was certainly, to some degree, nomadic. As I could find no reference to women coming here from India, our fellow Brits were an all-male domain. Certainly, there were mentions of Sikhs. By far and wide the majority of "Hindoo" hawkers were Muslim – or "Mohammedans", the then common name in circulation. On one occasion I actually read, "The Mohammedans call themselves Muslims." Unless quoting directly from the Advertiser or the Independent, I shall use Muslim.

There are, of course, reports of Afghani cameleers in Market Street from the 1850's. Before the coming of the railways, both camel and bullock teams were the best way to transport goods over long distances, albeit slowly.

The camel's advantage was that it could go for many days without needing to drink water. When Bendigo was linked to Melbourne by rail in 1862, it would close an important source of trade to those very slow-moving teams. The Afghans and their noble ships of the desert would find fame in the more arid colonies, even though they were disliked by the Europeans there.

In the Bendigo Advertiser of 3rd April 1862, a report from the Eaglehawk Police Court gives us a rare insight into early multicultural Bendigo. This case involved someone named "Singo, a negro" who abused Mary Farrell, "a single woman living with John Mahomet, a Hindoo". Singo, possibly Afro American (I am guessing here), threatened to "anatomise the larynx and heart of Mary Farrell" who was probably Irish born. Mr Mahomet, being labelled a "Hindoo" may have been Indian or possibly from Afghanistan. The Advertiser reported: "The Bench, not choosing to rely on the unsupported testimony of the lady, dismissed the case". I feel sure that the lady's choice of company went against her in this case and "living in sin" with a Hindoo relegated her in the moral eyes of the Court.

The Advertiser of Friday 20th October 1865 reported the death of Victoire Ryley, who had died from burns when the White Hills hut she shared with her husband ignited. The deceased woman's husband was described as "a Hindoo and a Mohammedan". The couple may or may not have been legally married, certainly not an Islamic marriage as there were no Imams available.

Under the existing British law of the day, if a female British Subject married a man of a different nationally, regardless of religion, then the woman would be legally regarded as having the nationality of her husband. Simple as that folks. I feel that particular law was designed to discourage the ladies form running off with a foreigner – they would lose the British status.

Also, from the 1860's, the Advertiser reported on Saturday, 12th January 1867, that "a Hindoo miner, Beenac Johns, fell down a mine shaft at Ironbark yesterday, broke his collarbone," which was set at the hospital. It is not possible to determine this gentleman's religious faith, but this does indicate that a very small number of other nationalities were still mining for gold.

It is at this point that the Indian population of Bendigo drops off the radar for over a decade, which gives us the opportunity to have a quick look at the three main religions of the Sub-Continent.

What we call Hinduism is actually a broad umbrella term given to a variety of religious, cultural, social, political and philosophical beliefs, which have their origin in the Vedic religion of the Aryans.

The Aryans were Europeans, very ancient ones of course. The Universal Soul, or Brahmann, is uncreated, limitless and eternal. Brahmann is the subtle essence within the universe and the innermost soul of each individual.

With a foundation in having many lifetimes, a person's karma, or spiritual credit or debt, will determine the course of the next lifetime. Spiritual liberation comes via knowledge, kind actions and spiritual devotion. With many deities, religious texts and rituals, it is a big religion. One of the most important festivals is Diwali – or Festival of Lights. Traditionally Hindus are cremated, the ashes being spread on the Ganges River.

The Sikh faith was founded by Guru Nanak in the northern Indian province of Punjab, which was culturally divided by Hindus and Muslims. Guru Nanak was the first of ten Guru's, or Teachers, of the Sikh faith. Sikh men grow their hair long, wrapping it in a turban.

Islam originated from a revelation given to the Prophet Mohammed 14 centuries ago. This occurred in a cave in the hills above Medina in present day Saudi Arabia. Muslims regard both Moses, Abraham and Jesus as Prophets of Islam, with Mohammed being the Final Prophet before Doomsday. Keep in mind that both the Jewish and Christian faiths believe in a day of divine judgement as well. What are called "The Five Pillars Of Islam" contain Fasting (Ramadan), Confession of the unity of God, Prayer (five times per day), Charity and Pilgrimage, Muslim men must make at least one pilgrimage to Mecca. Fridays are regarded as the most important day for communal prayer. Animals slaughtered for food must have a cleric present, reciting specific prayers. This food is called Halal, which had parallels with the Jewish Kosher – or blessed animal meat. Muslims are completely abstinate from alcohol.

Mahommedan Religious Service in Rosalind Park.

GROUPS OF WORSHIPPERS.

(Courtesy of the State Library of Victoria)

I hope all of that wasn't too confusing for you, although it was for me. Now we return to our narrative as brown skinned British Subjects started to appear on the streets of Bendigo.

When we speak of hawkers, or sellers, in the nineteenth century, we are describing those who would wander through the streets with their horse-drawn or human powered carts. Various items could be sold from the carts, whether it be clothing and fabrics, fruit and vegetables, or occasionally ice-cream. For our Indian friends, a horse-drawn cart would have been dreamt about – all references to their carts indicates they had to push them themselves. Research by Mr James Lerk indicated that the hawkers were funded by local solicitors. Clients of the solicitors would often allocate monies to their local legal eagle to invest on their behalf. They were, in our modern understanding, the micro-businesses of their day. Initially, there appears to have been very little concern about them, although some did have a reputation for being pushy. They had to make that sale!

India, at that time, had been regarded as "the Jewel in the Crown of the British Empire", no doubt surrounded by the gold from Bendigo. On Monday 26th May 1873, an Indian Exhibition opened at the Gromann's Post Office Chambers, View Point, with displays of Indian Zoology, including what was termed "Munghoores" or Mongoose. This exhibition was sponsored by the Acclimatisation Society, which had already introduced sparrows, blackbirds and so forth into the local area. At the time, serious consideration was given to introducing the Mongoose to Australia in an effort to reduce the numbers of snakes. It probably would have reduced the numbers of everything else as well. The exhibition drew good numbers, with the Advertiser noting "Although not a very large or imposing one, the exhibition is well worth a visit".

In the early 1880's, the number of Indian immigrants slowly began to climb, with the Advertiser of Thursday 24 July 1884 noting: "Yesterday was regarded by Mohammedans in the colony as a feast, or holy day, that of Ramzan". Obviously, the reporter/editor didn't quite understand that Ramadan is the start of a fast, from the sighting of the thirteenth new moon right through to the next new moon. Fasting from sun-up to sun-down, the fast is ended daily with what is called Iftar. For many decades, the press would refer to Ramadan as Razaman, which actually reflects a peculiar Indi-

an pronunciation. Unfortunately, July 1884 would see a turning point in attitudes to these men. The Advertiser of Monday 28th July would carry a news
report on an outbreak of smallpox in Forbes NSW. As the disease was en-
demic in parts of India, it was thought that the disease may "possibly have
been brought into the colony in the packs and goods vended door to door
by itinerant Mohammedan hawkers".

One of the earliest reports of Muslim hawkers printed in the Advertiser
is from the Court Notice section, Thursday 2nd October 1884. Described as
being "a Hindoo" and "a Mohammedan", a hawker named Ibrahim was subject to a worthless cheque for an exchange of goods by one Thomas Eager.
On day one of the trial against Eager, it was discovered that Ibrahim could
not speak English, just like the other Muslim men who accompanied him.
Ibrahim made it quite clear he could only swear an oath on the Qur'an of
which the Court didn't have a copy. The trial was adjourned until the next
day. This time a Muslim hawker who could speak English arrived with Ibrahim also carrying a copy of the Islamic holy book. The Court witnessed what
was regarded as a Muslim oath and "finding it solemn enough" accepted it
as being legally valid. I shall leave it to the Advertiser's report of the 3rd of
October to tell what happened next. "He (Ibrahim) turned over one page
and continued to read from the next. The court waxed impatient, and upon
the witness turning over another page and still continuing to read...An alter-
cation then ensued between the interpreter, the witness and the bench".
No reason is given as to why Ibrahim continued to read from the Qur'an and
the case was adjourned until the next day. Thomas Eager was found guilty of
issuing a worthless cheque to Ibrahim, with a prison sentence of three
months being imposed upon him, the first week being in solitary confine-
ment.

I found it quite interesting, while reading the online Advertisers from the
1880's and 1890's, just how much space was given over to explaining the
Islamic faith. Some articles seemed to be quite academic in approach, others
more comparative with the Christian faith – Christianity being the more superior of course.

The Indian hawker population seemed to be renters rather than owners.
A house in the then named Dowling Street (Hopetoun Street), was a popular

rental property for both Muslim and Sikh hawkers. Although of different faiths, they had all come from the Punjab and, as we shall see, some had been members of the British Army, so they had much in common. The Hawkers rented other properties, Specimen Cottage being a rental for them in the early 1890's. This put them in close proximity to the Jewish Synagogue and the notorious red-light district of Bernal Street – nicely renamed Chapel Street.

The main items sold by the hawkers from their carts in the 1880's appears to have been solidly clothing and accessories. An emphasis was put on women's clothing, although items for men and children were available. This trend would change to fruit or ice cream vending once the Depression of the 1890's started to bite. Outcries from local greengrocers about unfair competition from the hawkers exploded in the Letters to the Editors page. Some local residents were solidly against the hawkers, some supported their initiative and the opportunity to buy cheaper fruit!

The hawkers found themselves confronted by police action from time to time, over what we would call alleged parking infringements relating to their carts. These legal actions were quite common, suggesting that the local police were perhaps targeting this non-European group deliberately. Each infringement was heard at the Police Court. In August of 1890, the Advertiser reported of "5 or 6" Hindoo fruit sellers" being brought before the court charged with "obstructing the public thoroughfare." Some local fruit shops proprietors had alerted the police to this nuisance, oddly enough. The magistrate dismissed the case, with the suggestion that if there was a problem then the Council should frame an appropriate by-law.

The Advertiser of Tuesday, 2nd December 1890, ran an article on the arrest of a "Hindoo" hawker, with the stunning title of: "A DRUNKEN HINDOO". It appears that the previous evening, in Dowling (Hopetoun) Street, Constable Farrar arrested a hawker named Budda Sing on a charge of being drunk and disorderly. I have used the reported spelling here – Singh would be correct, indicating that he was a Sikh. Incidentally, like Muslims and Hindus, Sikhs should avoid alcohol too. Leaving it to the Advertiser: "Sing has the distinction of being the first Hindoo that has ever occupied a cell in the local watch house, where from time to time representatives from nearly every nationality on the globe have found their way". It is unknown if the man was on his way to the longest serving residence of the hawkers, or if he had been expelled by them due to his drunken condition. "Sing" would be locked up a number of times over the next few years because of his thirst.

The following week, all hawkers had to reapply for their annual licences at the Court of Petty Sessions, then held at the Bendigo Town Hall. On the bench was the Mayor, J.R.Hoskins with two assisting Justices of the Peace, A. Bayne and C. Roeder. Sergeant Fahey of the local police would vet the applicants to see if they were suitable. As the Advertiser of the 10th December reported, several Englishmen and one Chinese had applied as well "as about 80" Indians. Later reports dropped this number of 68. The sheer number of "Hindoo" applicants put the wind up the Bench. Mayor Hoskins was of the opinion, "that licences should not be granted in such a wholesale way to the Hindoos, who would overrun the country." The JP's agreed. Sergeant Fahey reported that nothing was "known" about 14 of the applicants, who had applied for licences the previous year. Fahey recommended they be granted renewals, while the others had come from both Melbourne and Ballarat and should be refused. Fahey would observe that: "The whole of the applicants, with few exceptions, have a military appearance, and have, I would image, served in some military force". My own research indicates that some of these men, along with some resident Muslim hawkers, had been members of the British Army's famed Bengal Lancers – cavalry regiments famous in their day for courageous acts while under fire. More about this later. Certainly, most of this group at the Licensing Court were perhaps Sikh, although some were definitely Muslim.

The Court would reject most of the applications, but not before an "intelligent, young Hindoo" spoke up: "But we are not like Chinese. We belong to Queen Victoria. All the same England, India and Australia. Queen Victoria rule over us. We are no Chinese". The Culture of Empire was not just limited to European British people by the looks of it, but the looks of the Indian British subjects did not please the Court.

The men decided to appeal the decision, with the next hearing held just two days before Christmas. Local Barrister, Mr Rymer Jr appeared for Mahomet Ali, clearly a Muslim gentleman. Rymer stated that if licences were granted, the men would leave Bendigo and would be able to hawk goods around Victoria The Bench stated that it would adhere to its original decision. The hawkers decided to forward a petition to the Governor of Victoria.

Another hearing was held on Wednesday 7 January 1891. The hawkers petition had found its way to Premier James Munro. Despite pleas from the now un-licensed hawkers that they would starve or be forced to "commit rash acts", the Premier, replied to the Advertiser's Melbourne Correspondent, that he could do nothing as licenses were a matter for magistrates. Mr Munro also indicated that he had communicated with the Indian government, arguing that: "...this class of emigration to Australia should be restricted."

Once again, the local Bench upheld its original decision. We do know the identity of one of the hawkers in this legal battle, namely Khoda Rahim, also he is also referred to as Khodabux Rahimbux, or even H.M. Rabimbux. The "bux" or "bx" was often applied to the hawkers whether they be Hindu, Muslim or Sikh. Mr Rahim was from the Punjab, living at Specimen Cottage well into 1892. In 1896, he was in Melbourne working as a draper. He appears to have had military experience, for he left Australia in 1901 and joined to Somaliland Supply and Transport Corps in Africa, serving three years in that unit. My thanks to Barbara Poustie of the Bendigo Historical Society for this information.

By August 1891, concerns over Indian migration were being raised in the Victorian Parliament and in the other colonies as well. Unlike the trickle of Chinese now entering the colonies, the Indians were British subjects, most who swore absolute allegiance to Her Majesty and the Empire.

Not everyone saw these subjects of Her Majesty as a threat, although we can see them as being minority voices. The Bendigo Independent on Monday 13th February 1893, reported on a suggestion for the upcoming Easter Fair: "Mr Palmer, of the No 1 Fire Brigade is trying to arrange for the turning out of Hindoos in their oriental dress, etc, in the Easter Fair procession in a similar style of the Chinese. One of them by the name of Derahkaham, is to go to Melbourne to interview the Hindoos there with the object of getting them to take part". It was reported that the Indians were quite enthused. Unfortunately, the detailed reports of the 1893 procession do not mention any "Hindoos" whatsoever, so we can assume that they didn't, or were not permitted to, take part at all.

In line with other newspapers further afield, the Advertiser began a campaign against what was called "the Asiatic Invasion". From the Editorial of Monday 4th September 1893, we read: "The influx of Hindoos, Syrians, Pathans and Afghans into the colony is becoming a question for serious consideration. So long as only a few were to be seen about little notice was taken of them...Their manners, customs and religion are so foreign and repugnant to those of the British population of the country that a strong feeling of antagonism is certain to result". Like other papers, the Advertiser called for restricting immigration, noting that steps had been taken against Chinese immigrants.

On Saturday 23rd September 1893, an Editorial lists "11 different castes of tribes", quite "exclusive of Chinese". Apart from those previously mentioned, the colony also had populations of Lingalese, Madrasees, Scindees, Bengalees, Creoles, Assyrians, Sikhs, Moguls and Seedees." The Editorial ends with: "If the country is not to be inundated with these people it will be necessary to restrict the number arriving by the seaboard, just as the Chinese are restricted". To justify its position, the Advertiser had commented negatively about them, allegedly living in high density numbers, the threat of disease, their poverty and manners.

And so, it went on – right to 1901. I was quite shocked at the campaign against "the Asiatics" with the local press following the sentiments reported in Melbourne and elsewhere. It also appeared to me that the same claims are still being made against some non-European groups in some of the media and by more "right wing" political groups. I have heard similar comments made by some local residents as well.

In 1894, a comment by Mr A.S. Bailes, MLA, at a Bendigo Town Hall meeting of the Women's Franchise Movement gives an indication of the sentiment of the times. Dr Quick was also at the meeting, held in support of women getting the right to vote. The Advertiser of Tuesday 24th July 1894 quotes the local MLA; "Had not their mothers, wives, daughters and sisters as much a right to vote as the dirty, turbaned Hindoo or Chinaman?" A male member of the audience yelled "No!" and Mr Bailes replied that he was sorry to hear that.

Attacks against the hawkers began occurring throughout the colony, including one reported assault here in Bendigo. The Independent of Friday 1st February 1895 reported under the headline – "A Hindoo Hawker Assaulted and Robbed" – "Mahomet Eli, ice cream seller, selling ice cream in Lily Street, New Chum, opposite the New Chum Hotel, was assaulted and robbed by four men, who were later apprehended." The men had come out of the hotel and bought four ice creams which were given to nearby children. Unprovoked, they set upon the vendor, punching him and tearing his coat, and making off with what money he had. The Advertiser would give the man's name as Mohammed Eli – although it was probably Ali – indicating that he would have been Muslim. The attackers were brought to trial, found guilty and sentenced to prison. Although alcohol would have played a part here, the ramping up of fear-based reports of "the invasion" found a home in the fearful hearts of some local residents. This still goes on today when we hear of abuse and even violence against Muslims, Indians and African people in the community.

And the physical attacks continued, even when there was little evidence of migrants committing any offense at all.

Our local Muslim hawkers seemed to have been under a bit of pressure within their ranks, for a small group of men they had a number of legal actions against each other, mostly for monies allegedly owed by one against the another. One lawsuit involved the delivery of what was the grandparent of all sheep – far too big and heavy for them to lift for the purposes for ritual slaughter – a clear reference to Halal – which the men had to conduct themselves, as no Imam was present

In the Advertiser of Wednesday 19th August 1896, a fairly lengthy article appeared under the title "A Modammendan's Funeral". I shall give a summary of the Muslim funeral of Cheda Khan, although the name given in the article states Chedu Friedbux. Cheda Khan was originally from Punjab in northern India. Having been in the colony for six or seven years, he had died in the hospital the previous Saturday from Pneumonia. Usually, according to Islamic tradition, deceased people are buried within 24 hours, so the delay of three days remains unexplained. From the house in Hopetoun Street, the coffin, draped in white, was carried on the shoulders of fellow Muslims along Lyttleton Terrace, then Mitchell and Carpenter Streets to Bendigo cemetery. No small feat by the way. Arriving at the chapel, the coffin was placed on the ground at the rear, with the mourners removing their shoes for an hour-long Islamic funeral. The grave site, which is in the Anglican section, had been dug in a traditional Christian way, for the feet to be pointed east, with the slightly wider areas for the head facing west. In Islamic tradition, the head faces east, so cemetery staff had to widen that part of the grave. To bide their time, the Advertiser noted the Muslims sat in a circle smoking cigarettes, "but otherwise observing due decorum".

When the white linen was removed from the coffin, "His countrymen, from religious scruples, objected to the plate and ornaments on the coffin and they were consequently removed". When the lid of the coffin was removed to allow a final viewing, other people in the cemetery "moved by a morbid spirit of curiosity eagerly thronged round the coffin, and it was with difficulty that Plain Clothes Constable Haigh, who was unofficially present, could keep them back to as to allow of the friends carrying out their funeral arrangements without due influence". After more prayers, the grave was filled in by the mourners, who gave dates and other fruits to the crowd of gawkers. Before leaving the century, the Sextant, Mr Redpath, was given the linen with the instruction to give it to someone who might need it.

It is interesting to note the reason why this Muslim burial was permitted in Anglican Christian ground. There is simply no record of it at the Anglican Cathedral, so perhaps permission was granted "just this once" because Cheda Khan was a British subject. Most Muslim burials, especially at White Hills cemetery, took place amongst the Chinese burials, which was something the very British Muslims objected to. In regard to Cheda Khan's funeral, it seems that a plain clothes policeman just happened to be present at the cemetery, in an "unofficially present" way of course.

By 1898, the storm clouds against non-European immigration were about to burst forth. With Constitutional Conventions underway to establish a Federation of the colonies, the press made one salient point very clear. The next extract is from the Independent, Saturday 28th May 1898, under the heading: "The Indian Influx". The Editorial, after a tirade of fear against the Indians in case they brought in Cholera, Smallpox and the Bubonic Plague, ended with, "One of the first matters to be seriously taken in hand by the Federal Parliament of Australia should be the influx of Asiatics".

In July 1898, the Victorian Parliament saw the introduction of the Immigration Restriction Bill, which we might call the White Victoria Policy. Its aim was to check the influx of "Hindoos and Afghans" as well as other Asians. A Dictation Test of 50 English words, by any English author, was proposed, with the would-be immigrant having to write them down word perfect. Paupers would be excluded, as well as anyone who might become one in the future. Other exclusions would apply to those suffering "an infectious or contagious disease of a loathsome or dangerous character', and those convicted of serious crimes. The Advertiser, very supportive of the Bill, gave some interesting statistics on Friday 15th July 1898. Citing the population of Victoria in the 1850's, out of 450,000 people, some 42,000 were Chinese. In 1898, the total population of Victoria was put at 1.7 million people, of which 10,900 were "Asiatics". Hardly an invasion I should think. Despite that, the Bill easily passed the Lower House but was rejected in the Upper House. The Independent went so far as to blame the defeat of the popular Bill on the lobbying of Melbourne ship owners and agents. It also urged that fees for hawkers' licenses be "substantially increased", so as to discourage further immigration. Just three years later, more than the skeleton of the Victorian Bill would be introduced into Federal Parliament.

To wind up this lengthy chapter, I feel it is important to mention that a religious freedom was extended to Bendigo's earlier Muslim population, early in that halcyon year of 1901.

Prior to 1901, at the end of the Ramadan fast, the Muslim men of Bendigo would travel by train to Melbourne to celebrate Eid – sometimes called the Islamic Christmas, as it is a day of celebration and gift giving. On Friday 18th January 1901 – with the Commonwealth of Australia being the youngest nation on earth – the Town Clerk received a letter from Hadji Bunna Charley, asking for permission to use Rosalind Park for a service at 10.00am. The Mayor interviewed Mr Charley and others to ascertain what that service would entail. Quite satisfied that it was harmless, permission was granted for the service to be held on Tuesday, January 22nd. Unfortunately, there was some confusion over whether the new moon had arrived, as not all the Muslim men had seen it. To be sure, the Eid service was held over to the next day, Wednesday 23rd January 1901. The men had fasted for around 17 hours per day – long hot Bendigo summer days. The Advertiser mentioned that as now there were around 31 of them, this justified them having a local celebration, rather than travelling to Melbourne as they had previously done.

The "priest" as termed by the Advertiser, was Munshee Golam Mohammed, who read from the Qur'an on a small box in front of him. All of those present wore traditional white clothing common to the Punjab in that era. The service went for around 45 minutes, keenly observed by a large number of non-Muslim onlookers. The Advertiser's weekly pictorial, the Bendigonian, would publish two photographs of the event a fortnight later. There were no reports of any heckling or abuse from the non-Muslim crowd of onlookers. The service concluded with the men clasping hands with Mr Mohammed.

At that point, the Town Clerk approached the head man with some important news – Queen Victoria has passed away. Mr Mohammed is recorded as saying: "The very good Queen we all love; she is dead. All Kings and Queens must die, but never such a good Queens as ours, has died. We are indeed very sorry". The Muslim worshippers bowed their heads and expressed grief at the news. Despite the news that would sadden many, the Muslim men distributed fruit and lollies to the onlookers before walking out of the Park.

Muslims did have some support in the community, mostly because they avoided alcohol. In the nineteenth and early twentieth centuries, the Temperance Societies would hold that component of the Islamic faith quite high. On page one of the Independent of Thursday 7th March 1901, an article by "Rambler" would support the Muslim approach to good health by food, exercise and spiritual practice: "What amount of drugs and medicines we wonder would be required in more civilised communities if the resident were as temperate, abstemious, cleanly and active as the Arabs." No doubt "Mr Rambler" was a member of the Temperance Society and no doubt he also believed in the supremacy of "more civilised communities", i.e.: the British!

This won't be the last word on non-Christian people in Bendigo, in fact far from it. Let's take a look at a popular Bendigo institution that missed its own 150th birthday due to a rampaging virus named COVID 19.

CHAPTER EIGHT

A VERY BENDIGO FAIR.

Processions, parades and fairs of all sorts have been a common occurrence throughout human history and culture. Whether based on religious rituals and celebrations, historical anniversaries, or even political pursuits, processions form an important part of the cultural fabric of any society. The origins of the Bendigo Easter Fair (now Festival), were based in charity – to raise funds for the Hospital and Benevolent Asylum. It is an ongoing, traditional part of the social and cultural life of Bendigo. From my own perspective, after being away from Bendigo for 19 years, I returned in 2013, just missing the Easter Festival by a few days. It wasn't until Easter of 2014 that I felt I had really returned to Bendigo – keep in mind that I'm originally from East Preston.

A committee made up from members of various community groups met in 1870 to plan a fund-raising Fair for Easter of 1871. Notably, the Fair would begin on Easter Monday, after the very holy days of Good Friday and Easter Sunday. A procession of various community groups – cultural associations, friendly societies, which were in effect welfare societies for members, the local cavalry unit and local brass and highland bands would open the Fair. An invitation to the Governor was made, with the Governor accepting.

On Monday 10th April 1871, the Easter Fair opened with the arrival of the Governor, who made his way from the station to the balcony of the Shamrock Hotel. The procession then got underway. Following the procession was a Fancy Bazaar where there were stalls, raffles, a wheel of fortune and other entertainment. The Advertiser would comment, "Yesterday will long be re-membered as one of the greatest gaieties ever passed in Sandhurst, gaiety that was devoted to the best of purposes – to feed the hungry, clothe the naked, and heal the sick". The Fair was a great success and the Advertiser hoped it would continue – hope springs eternal here.

And it would continue, with many twists and turns, ongoing 150 years later. What follows is a summary of the Easter Fair from its inception in 1870 through to 1900 – it gives us a valuable insight into cultural practices, mis-understandings and even challenges.

In 1872, with the Fair still in its infancy, some Bendigonians were af-fronted by a special cricket match – a cricket match played by two all-female teams. The women cricketers wore ankle length skirts with either a blue or scarlet shirt. Cricket, an English import of great importance to the male population, was regarded solely as a male domain. This "insult" to masculine sovereignty, although meant to be a novelty, was the very first women's cricket match played in Australia.

Another "novelty", as reported by the Advertiser on Friday 21st March 1879, would be the inclusion of a "Chinese Carnival" in the Fair. Some 15 tons of paraphernalia would be imported by the Chinese – banners, cos-tumes, chariots, armaments, lanterns and so forth. The 1879 procession would see the Chinese parading in the body of the parade – the tradition of making up the rear was yet to be established. With 250-300 members, it was probably made up from some local Chinese residents – this would sub-sequently change. Chinese Opera and cultural displays were conducted in the Chinese Exhibition building at the then Showgrounds, currently the Tom Flood Sports Centre. Large attendances at evening shows were reported.

It would be incorrect to assume that the Chinese took part in every East-er procession since 1879. On other occasions, the Chinese were late to very late, effectively having their own procession long after the official parade had ended. At first, the local news media looked kindly upon this, given that Chinese from Ballarat, Melbourne and Beechworth would arrive by train on Easter Monday to augment the local Chinese contingent. The train some-times arrived late. It was also noted that the Bendigo Chinese took great pride in their offerings, with lengthy preparations being made at the Ironbark Camp before they embarked for the city centre. Over time, however, the local media became very critical of the Chinese, given that parade goers were often disappointed by the late arrival or a no-show at all.

Despite all of this, the Chinese involvement was highly appreciated by most Bendigonians – rather unusual as the Chinese were largely shunned every other day of the year. The first appearance of the Chinese in 1879 was rewarded with a banner from the Easter Fair Committee, a banner proudly carried in the procession for years afterwards. The Chinese would also provide fireworks for the Fair, being granted 50 pounds towards costs.

The Advertiser's report of the 1882 procession gives us an insight into the views held about the Chinese and their importance in the parade: "And poor John Chinaman, after all the poor fellow is very much of a human being, that is he has a good deal of our common nature in him. When a subject is properly laid before him by his European superiors, and it is shown to him that in the exercise of virtue which we call charity, he can make a common purpose with us, he is not backward. It is not the first time the Chinese have made their portion of the Easter Fair the most attractive of any…".The Advertiser also mentioned that around 30,000 people watched the 1882 procession, with the official statistics that half of Bendigo's population was under nineteen years of age. We can assume that most of these youngsters would be locally born.

In 1885, the Advertiser detailed a float provided by the Golden Square Fire Brigade, featuring three young children. The only name given was Sissy Montgomery, who was dressed as the "Goddess of Plenty", perhaps "Fortune" would be a more appropriate here. Beside her was a small boy dressed as a miner. An aboriginal boy sat behind them "…in his hands native implements of war…". To quote the Advertiser's description "The aboriginal was placed at the rear, he being supposed to have made room for the advancement of civilisation, which was represented by the miner and the Goddess of Plenty…". It is quite possible that the unknown aboriginal boy was a local Dja Dja Wurrung, put in his place at the rear of the float indicating his assumed inferiority.

And the band continued to play on. The 1886 Fair hosted an "All Nations" Bazaar which was held at the Masonic Hall in View Street. Similar bazaars, with parades, had already been held in Melbourne. The "All Nations" Bazaar was somewhat limited to those nations that held empires – the United Kingdom, America, France, Germany, Spain and Turkey, with an Australian stall thrown in for good measure. There was nothing about the Chinese or local First Nation people included in the Bazaar.

Fair goers were met with a series of national displays including flags, paintings and stalls staffed by people in national costume. Both the Spanish and Turkish sections were staffed by Anglo-Celtic ladies. The stalls were stocked with a host of donated items, including paintings, toys, lacework, cushions, plates, lanterns, vases and various household items. I was a bit surprised to read that the German stall, run by two ladies both named Ms Roeder, had a French marble clock for sale. Certainly, a mix of cultures here, maybe. All proceeds went to the Hospital and Asylum.

In 1892, the Chinese would outdo themselves with a massive Imperial Dragon, imported from China directly to Bendigo. This dragon was called "Dragon" in the Cantonese language common to the Bendigo Chinese – "Loong".

Dragons of various sorts had long been part of Eastern and Western traditions, although with quite substantial differences. In the Western tradition, dragons had been seen as being hungry monsters, devouring sheep, cattle, people and anything else in their path. Gold sovereigns, common in Bendigo once upon a time, had a profile of Queen Victoria on one side, with St George slaying a dragon on the other. The dragon in question looks quite small, probably because gold sovereigns were not all that big either. In the Eastern tradition, dragons were a symbol of abundance, strength and vitality. Regarded as being vegetarian and somewhat deaf, the ceremonial dragons had to be kept awake with firecrackers – lots of them! Also, dragons began their lives as cod fish, who might be able to swim through a mystical portal called the Dragon's Gate and be transformed into a dragon. The arrival of Loong in the 1892 Easter Procession gives us an idea of the cultural differences between Europeans and Chinese.

The Chinese marched from the Ironbark Camp to the marshalling area at Market Square, carrying Loong over some considerable distance. This was done with great ceremony and reverence. The Bendigo Advertiser gives a good (European) description of Loong's first appearance: "...came a mighty dragon nearly a hundred yards long, with a fearful looking head and spikey tail...to the intense delight of the onlookers...The dragon has a terribly ugly head, with great spreading horns, and one golden horn projecting out of his forehead. He had fierce, glaring eyes...a terrible monster...". Not exactly a glowing report from the Advertiser which also added that "... people scattered from its wriggling tail...." The following year, the Bendigo Independent would describe Loong in similar terms. "The dragon had a fierce appearance. His head was unspeakably ugly." Beauty is always in the eyes of the beholder!

Despite being quite unattractive to the European eye, Loong would establish a pivotal place in the Easter Procession for almost the next 80 years and continues to sleep on at the Golden Dragon Museum, although most of his colour has now faded due to the passage of time. Loong is the oldest existing imperial dragon in the world due to the 'Cultural Revolution' in China during the mid-1960's. Under Chairman Mao, who wanted to revamp his personal power, all the old links to the Imperial Dynasties, including the dragons, were destroyed along with many people as well.

As much as Loong and its Chinese keepers were valued at Easter, there were other drums beating throughout the land. These drums sounded the rising of an Australian nationalism, imperial at its core and fearfully racist as well. There was to be no doubt that this was a British nation and it was going to stay that way.

CHAPTER NINE

ONE NATION, ONE PEOPLE, ONE DESTINY.

As indicated in the previous chapter, by 1882 half of Bendigo's population were under 19 years of age, born in the colony and physically distant from the home countries of their parents. This was occurring around the continent and was inevitable. Under the process known as accent levelling, a distinctive Australian accent was developing, no doubt to the dismay of some older people. A blending of cultures was underway, with a leaning towards British tastes in food, sports and clothing. The Germans, for example, have had no interest in adopting cricket as a national sport, yet on the cricket pitches of Bendigo, the sons of German immigrants would take up the sport with gusto. They started to see themselves as "Australians" alongside those from other parental heritages as well. Although still very British, the native born began to do and see things a bit differently, establishing a new identity and taking pride in it.

One of the earliest forms of a new identity appeared in Rosalind Park in 1860, with a game of football that had no proper rules, no goal posts and was played over two weekends – this was an early form of what would become Australian Rules Football. Very much a Victorian institution, New South Wales would stay loyal to the very British Rugby.

The inauguration of the Australian Natives Association (ANA) would propel a nationalist agenda, with a Bendigo branch being established in 1874.

The ANA made slow progress at first, with the Bendigo chapter having just 17 members in 1882. However, this would change as nationalist momentum grew in the 1880's and 1890's, fuelled by fears of Asian migration to the colonies. The widely read "Bushman's Bible" – the Bulletin – would also promote a national identity through its pages, with stories and poems by A.B "Banjo" Patterson, Henry Lawson, and "Steele Rudd" (A.H. Davis) to name just a view. These authors developed an identity built on the "bush" – wattles instead of daffodils, damper instead of scones, small struggling selectors instead of baronial estates. The Bulletin was also solidly anti-Chinese. The call for the colonies to federate into one British nation grew louder as the years of the nineteenth century ticked away. The first nationalist day of celebration took place on Thursday 26th of January 1888. This day, named Foundation Day, had been celebrated in New South Wales for a number of years. As it was a centenary, all capital cities observed the official proclamation of 1788 declaring that all land in the new British settlement was hereafter a colony of Britain. The Advertiser reported that some members of the Bendigo ANA would be going to Melbourne to take part in the proceedings. The Advertiser's report also gives us an insight into the views of British sovereignty and the status of First Nation People. "As far we know, the first people who landed on our shores were a party of Dutch sailors, who accidentally came across the northern coast of Australia in 1606, but when several of their comrades were killed by the blacks, the rest became dismayed and took their departure, never to return". Obviously, according to the newspaper, "the blacks" were not real people – certainly outcasts in their own countries, unable to vote and not counted in any colonial census. Although still quite physically visible, they were officially "invisible" people legally. This anniversary, along with the Tenterfield Address given by Henry Parkes, would fuel nationalist sentiment and a push for Federation.

By the mid 1880's immigration to the colonies and places like Bendigo had slowed. Most immigrants were still largely British, although Bendigo was graced when a number of Spanish families arrived and began growing commercial crops of tomatoes in various parts of the Bendigo area. For around sixty years, tomatoes would be grown and sent by train to Melbourne.

In 1890's Bendigo – it was renamed Bendigo in 1891 after a poll voted against keeping the official name of Sandhurst any longer – life appeared to be good to most people. Although the Depression of the early 1890's had seen bank closures and a drifting of some young people to Melbourne, the cultural life of Bendigo flourished. With a variety of stage performances, including American author Mark Twain giving two lectures in 1895, a very robust Easter Fair, band recitals in the parks and the first demonstration of moving pictures in the Temperance Hall in November 1896, Bendigonians could still enjoy a very European styles of living.

Something that would cause more than a ripple was what today we would call the status of women. Women have traditionally been the home-makers, the shop keepers and the mainstay of domestic servants for the wealthy. Following the rise of female activists pushing for the right to vote in Britain and the United States, on May 10th, 1894, a society was formed in Bendigo for the extension of the vote to women. Some men found this a preposterous idea, indeed an affront to their masculine supremacy. Fortunately, with male supporters such as Dr John Quick on board locally, the right for women to vote was won within a decade. In its interesting to note that at this time women found it fashionable to wear dresses with what was called a Bustle – a pad or framework worn at the back to fill out the rear, very fully I might add.

The 1890's saw an explosion in technology, first with a battery-operated tramway which soon became a steam powered tramway due to flat batteries. The telephone arrived along with electric street lighting in Pall Mall and View Street. Bendigo, along with other prosperous communities, embraced the new technologies that hailed from Europe and America.

The push for a federation of the colonies was agreed to by the colonial Premiers, with groups of lawyers and politicians putting together a new system of government with an intricate Constitution that would have to be agreed upon by voters Australia wide. Although very much the British Westminster style of government, the constitutionalists borrowed heavily from the United States. There would be two houses of parliament, not a House of Commons and a House of Lords, but rather a House of Representatives and a Senate. There would not be a president but rather a Governor-

General who would represent Her Majesty federally, just as the Governors did at a colonial level. From Federation, the colonies would be renamed as States.

Bendigo was massively pro-federation, with support from the Town Council and even the Anglican Church. The local newspapers were in full favour also. The reasons were quite apparent – a Federal Government could provide services such as defence and postal services much more effectively than the colonies on their own. It could also bring in uniform immigration laws, which was paramount to an increasingly fearful European population. Japan, once an isolated feudal society, had begun rapid modernisation from 1860 and was emerging as a major power in the Pacific. Although Chinese immigration into Vitoria had been severely restricted, Indians and other "Asiatics" continued to arrive. In Queensland, sugar cane farmers brought in South Sea Islanders to harvest the cane, slaves savagely removed from their own lands, similar to what had occurred throughout human history. In June of 1898, 95% of Bendigonian voters voted YES for Federation. Another poll that followed amendments to the Commonwealth Constitution Bill in 1899, returned a 98% YES vote.

In 1900, that Bill was presented in the British Houses of Parliament. The Bill passed easily and was sent to Queen Victoria for Royal Assent. It would be one of the last pieces of legislation she would ever sign. The date for the commencement of the Commonwealth of Australia was set as being January 1st, 1901. There were enormous celebrations in Bendigo and elsewhere. A new nation was being formed, although strongly within the boundaries of the British Empire. Australian by birth and British at heart. The focus and intention was clear – this was going to be a nation for white people only, to the exclusion of all others. The monoculturalists had won.

CHAPTER TEN

ADVANCE AUSTRALIA VERY FAIR

On 1st January 1901, the Commonwealth of Australia came into being, with the first sitting of Parliament held at Melbourne's Exhibition Buildings. Melbourne would be the provisional capital of Australia until a permanent one would be built, named Canberra. It would be 1927 before the new capital would become operational.

Bendigo was very much part of the official festivities in Melbourne. Although the Chinese were greatly disliked, it was felt that a Chinese representation should be made, and this was provided through an appearance by Loong – the Imperial Dragon of the Bendigo Chinese. Transported in sections on the train to Melbourne and then reassembled, the Little Bourke Street Chinese community made up the legs of this mighty symbol of Chinese culture. Loong would gain the honour of being the only existing relic from the Federation celebrations as the century wore on. Dr John Quick, the first Member for Bendigo in the new Parliament, would also be awarded the Imperial Honour of the Knight's Bachelor, making him Sir John Quick.

The new nation also found itself at war – the Dutch farmers of South Africa had tried to form their own state free of the British, which the British naturally refused. The Boers, as they were known, had already taken up arms and the Australian Colonies sent military detachments to fight for the British Empire. Some Bendigo based men found their way there, with some staying permanently as causalities of this war. The whole thing was made worse by the actions of the German Kaiser who openly supported the Boers' quest for independence.

Many dignitaries from around the Empire came to witness the formation of the new country. Afterwards, tours of notable places took place, with Bendigo being on the itinerary. A bit of an unfortunate stir was created at a luncheon held at the Town Hall, when some Muslim Cavalry Officers from India were guests of the Mayor. From the Advertiser of Thursday, 7th February 1901: "At the luncheon given by the Mayor of Bendigo, one of the officers of the Fifth Battalion unwittingly caused the Mohammedans to recoil in horror by offering ham sandwiches". Muslim's are prohibited from eating pork by the way.

The Victorian Census of 1901 gives us an idea of how small a number the non-Christians were in relation to an overall population of almost 2 million people. Anglicans came in at 424,052 adherents, with Roman Catholics numbering 263,712. Presbyterians were the third most numerous at 191,471 and Methodists with 180,281. Baptists were fifth at 13,935. Congregationalists, Salvation Army, Disciples of Christ and Unitarians made a combined total of 37,000. There was even an Australian Church numbering just 966 persons. Jewish adherents numbered 5,897 with Confucians, who would be Chinese, coming in at 3,389. Muslims numbered a rather small 467. Although 10,820 declined to state their religion and another 2,391 stated no religion at all, there are no figures for those who were Hindu or Sikh. Certainly, those who followed non-Christian religions (and were most likely to be non – European), made up a very small percentage of the Victorian population. Despite this apparent reality, the call for a restriction on non-European migration rose to a fever pitch.

Australia was just over three weeks old when news of the death of Queen Victoria was received from London. The then longest reigning Monarch had passed and the entire country went into a state of mourning. Queen Victoria had been the only monarch most people had ever known, so it was new territory for the loyal Britishers. I should think that every square centimetre of black material in Bendigo went into draping the Town Halls of Greater Bendigo and businesses as well. Some businesses are reported to have used Royal Purple draping. The official day for the memorial observation was set for Saturday 2nd February 1901, although the churches had held special services the previous Sunday. The Bendigo memorial consisted of a parade through the central streets, culminating at Rosalind Park. Participants in the procession included the 5th Victorian Army Battalion, cadets, rifle clubs, fire brigades, Friendly Societies, with Oscar Flight leading Northcotts's City Band who played a very solemn "Death March". An estimated 10,000 people gathered in Rosalind Park to sing the National Anthem, "God save the King", referring to the new Monarch, George the Fourth. Eaglehawk and Strathfieldsaye held their own memorials, with an estimated 2,000 to 8,000 people in Canterbury Park. A new nation indeed, but fiercely British.

In the winter of 1901, legislation was presented in the House of Representatives. It was entitled the Immigration Restriction Act and caused considerable concern in Britain and India. The Act was, for all intents and purposes, a carbon copy of the ill-fated Victorian Act of 1898. The Commonwealth Act required that all "coloured" immigration seekers would have to sit a dictation test, which could be in any European language, as well as having medical checks and checks to determine their good character (or not!). Residents "of colour" also had to apply for a special certificate to enter another state, a requirement of which was to submit to having their right hand printed like a fingerprint. From the British perspective, it meant that some British subjects, such as from India and Africa for example, would lose the freedom to migrate where they wished. In India, the realisation was that they were being targeted by their southern British Empire members. The Editorial in the Advertiser of Wednesday 18th September 1901 seems to sum it all up: "The desire for a "White Australia" may be regarded as practically unanimous. According to Mr Deakin, there are about 80,000 coloured aliens in Australia, of whom somewhat less than one-half are Chinese, apparently about 9,000 are Polynesians, while the rest are from a variety of people, mainly those of the neighbouring countries of Asia...Australia's great extent of territory, and her proximity to the teeming millions of Asia, make it imperative that stringent measures shall be taken to protect the Australian people from the influx of large numbers of the Asiatic and African races....".

Spelling it out, there was a great fear that Australian would be overrun by non-Europeans, a fear that still exists in some to this very day.

Despite being "practically unanimous", there were voices opposed to a White Australia, both locally and elsewhere. Sometimes their motives might be questioned, however, there was a spark here that would eventually be ignited into a fanned flame. In a letter to the Editor (Advertiser) Tuesday 22nd October 1901, a writer signing as "G.F.W.", identifying as a Christian, wrote: "The coloured man has as much right to occupy this God's Earth as the white man, else why did God place him here?" Sounds good, then G.F.W. continues; "I as a white man, naturally consider we are superior to the coloured races, but our duty should be to raise them up to our level, not seek to crush them down lower than they are by 'man's inhumanity to man' treatment". I wonder how G.F.W. felt about our local First Nation people, given they were regarded as being little more than flora and fauna and treated as such.

By the way, as indicated, 80,000 non Europeans in a country with nearly 7 million people is a very small percentage of the entire population. What was known as, and still is, the White Australia Policy was designed to keep Australia European and predominantly British forever.

Concerns by the British Government did force the new nation to add a small, very tight loophole to the legislation. This was in the form of a Certificate of Exemption, which allowed the Commonwealth to waive the strict requirements of the Act in some applications for immigration. Needless to say, such certificates were only granted if the Commonwealth regarded it as being in that very nebulous term, the National Interest.

The Act was passed and became law. For the residents of Bendigo and elsewhere, relief came in knowing that their little Britain was now safe from the "teeming millions of Asia – a fool's paradise really, as those millions in our region could not develop the trade networks that comes with a multicultural society. European immigration was pitifully small, denting any great leap forward as a regional player. The beginnings of what has been called "The Cultural Cringe" in Australia had been embedded and Bendigo began to shrink from its once illustrious persona.

CHAPTER ELEVEN

ROAST BEEF AND WATTLE

As the new twentieth century got underway, Bendigo began a decline from a great gold producer to a town dependent on its other local industries and the farms that surrounded it. Many young families and individuals headed for Melbourne, where job opportunities were greater. One by one the large gold mines were closing, leaving ponds of contaminated water and increasingly derelict mine buildings. The European population could, at least, rest assured that they were safe from "the Asiatic influx" often written about in the local press.

And what of the Chinese and other non-European residents of Bendigo? For the Chinese a slow decline in their number was underway – very few Chinese women were allowed into the former colonies, so the almost totally male population either married European women or would remain bachelors. Interracial marriage of any sort was more than frowned upon, especially by Europeans. A number of fires over the years at the Ironbark Camp saw Bridge Street become the centre for Chinese activities. Those fires also destroyed many cultural items belonging to the Chinese and, with good fortune associated with dragons, Loong would escape any harm.

It is possible that the Bendigo Chinese may have shown their collective displeasure at the Immigration Restriction Act, as they did not appear in the 1902 Easter procession. When I discovered this, the only reason I found in the media was that they "had been left out of this year's procession". This, I believe, was an assumption by the Advertiser for it appeared to be so. What was reported in the weeks leading up to the 1903 Easter Fair I found quite intriguing. Harry Marks and other members of the Easter Fair Society went to see Dr Lamsey and other Chinese community leaders about Chinese participation in the upcoming Fair, including the procession. Obviously, Marks and company wanted the Chinese to be involved and the Chinese so agreed. The 1903 Easter Fair began on Monday, 13th April and as the Advertiser somewhat sarcastically reported: "The Chinese, as usual, were late. But the delay of an hour and a half was well compensated for the display they made". The Chinese, being 90 minutes late, had their own procession.

There is no apparent record still existing of how our Indian hawker residents reacted to the new Act – they were proudly British subjects, yet as despised as the Chinese. The celebration of Eid continued in Rosalind Park, with Munshee Golam Mohammed officiating as Imam. For the years immediately after 1901, Muslim numbers at Eid were about 30, suggesting most stayed on in Bendigo. What did catch my eye was an appeal by Harry Marks, printed in both the Advertiser and the Independent, asking Bendigo residents to supply horses and riding equipment so that the Muslims could take part in the 1903 Easter procession as the Bengal Lancers. The Fair's Committee had received a letter from Mr C. Bunna Khan, asking for support. Mark's public appeal stated that the Muslims "could obtain uniforms" and that some members had been in the military, experiencing action under fire under the Union Jack, the flag of Great Britain. This strongly suggests that some of Bendigo's small Muslim population had been members of the famous Bengal Lancers – cavalry regiments noted for their heroic deeds in battle.

The Bengal Lancers were the cream of the British Army's Indian regiments, eventually spawning the subject for American, British and French films in the following decades. There were a number of regiments from the early 1800's right up to World War Two. A report that uniforms to be worn in the 1903 procession were white and red narrowed the identification of the actual regiment to the 13th (Duke of Connaught) Regiment of Bengal Lancers. This regiment, recruited from northern India, saw active service in Afghanistan in 1880 and thereafter in the North-East Frontier, the region now covered by Pakistan. I might be wrong, but it seems to tie in nicely with the fact that most of these men arrived in Bendigo during the 1880's and early 1890's – after their military service. Certainly, these men had the uniforms and knew how to ride horses, as well as the observation by Marks that some had seen combat. For Muslims, this might have been a display of their valued British-hood, as well as their displeasure at being "put in the same boat as the Chinese", something they were quite vocal about at times. When one of their number passed away, they were insulted when the body was buried in the Chinese section of the White Hills Cemetery.

Unfortunately, the request for horses seems to have been quite unsuccessful. Reading the rather descriptive accounts of the 1903 procession in both local papers, there is no mention of the Bengal Lancers appearing whatsoever. As much as the Lancers were famous in their day, it seems that nobody wanted to lend their horse, for a few hours, to a Muslim Indian hawker. Lest we forget.

The Jewish population, as least being European, were not particularly affected by the new law. However, the Jewish population of Bendigo would decline in the early 1900's, forcing the closure of the Hebrew school and ultimately the Synagogue itself. Apart from the older people shuffling off the mortal coil, as we all eventually do, some Jewish residents also followed the road to Melbourne, where a healthy Jewish population continued to flourish.

Although there was some stagnation in Bendigo during those years, there were some exciting developments. The aborted battery/steam trams of the 1890's were replaced with an electrical tram service in 1903. A slow but steady growth in technology, especially electronic, was underway. And then there was the motion picture – the movies or flicks as they were often called. When the ground-breaking "The Story of The Kelly Gang" was screened at the Royal Princess Theatre in February 1907, it was reported that "thousands" attended the screenings. It had also been announced that the Melbourne based producers would make a film about Bendigo. "Living Bendigo" as it was titled, was a documentary of scenes, people and activities of the day. Unfortunately, although "Living Bendigo" was made and widely screened, no print or fragment of the film is known to exist.

The widespread success of that first bushranger film, and the many to follow, indicates a rather peculiar aspect of what we might call Australian culture – the hero worship of notorious criminals. Ned Kelly stands above the rest as a champion of the oppressed, struggling small farmers, even more because of the suits of armour forged to protect against police bullets at what would be the demise of the Kelly Gang, the siege of Glenrowan in June 1880. One of the Kelly Gang's hostages, Michael Reardon, made his way to Bendigo and is buried in the Catholic section of the Bendigo Cemetery. For a fair proportion of the Australian population, a general contempt for formality and pomposity quickly developed. This would lead to what is known as "The Tall Poppy Syndrome", which means if someone makes a name for themselves, they are then likely to be personally attacked for doing so. This can definitely be seen as a flaw in the Australian psyche. The bushranger was seen as someone who "bucked the system", most of whom were either shot or hanged.

Michael Reardon's Headstone

Michael Reardon's Gravesite

The success of such films and the proliferation of bushranger books worried members of the Temperance Societies, who agitated against them. In 1911, Australia was the world's biggest producer of feature films, many with a strong Australian flavour. In 1912, bushranger films were banned, and Australian film production greatly slowed.

The importance of film is often overlooked in many histories. Australian films of the silent and early "talkies" eras displayed on screen mythic tales of selectors, squatters and working class urbanites struggling to make a living. In short, something that local audiences could identify with. Certainly, British films were paramount, with increasing production from the United States. In a very short time, Bendigonians would become familiar with America cowboys and "Indians", and less familiar with their own local First Nation people. Although rarely accurate in detail, the emergence of motion pictures gave locals eyes to the world outside of Bendigo, even if what they saw was still steeped in stereotypical viewpoints of European superiority above all others. American culture began to creep into what had been a fiercely British society. Bendigo was still loyal to the Empire, but the emerging powerhouse of the United States was making inroads indeed.

In the years from 1901 to 1914, Bendigo seemed to just sit on a couch and quietly enjoy itself as best it could. The boom years were now just a memory for the shrinking number of people who were in Bendigo in the 1850's, 1860's and 1870's. These Bendigonians so opposed to the Chinese and other people from Asia, could rest assured that no more would be allowed into the country, thereby allaying their fears. In many ways, those years allowed a false sense of security to set in – British to the back teeth, but with an Australian accent and manner to upset the "Poms". As 1913 became 1914, little did anyone realise just what horrors were about to be unleashed in far-away Europe – and how thousands of Bendigonians would rush headlong into it.

CHAPTER TWELVE

FOR GOD, KING AND COUNTRY.

From the death of Queen Victoria in early 1901 to the outbreak of hostilities in Europe in August 1914, much had changed in the world and in Australia itself. Russia had suffered a humiliating defeat by the Japanese in 1905 and then experienced a revolution, which was quashed, in the very same year. Powered aviation became a reality, to the amazement of many. A nationalist revolution in China in 1911 had ended centuries of Imperial rule – and the queue, or pigtails, imposed upon Chinese men disappeared for all time. Europe would be divided into two opposing camps by treaties, Britain, France and Russia in one camp and Germany, the Austro-Hungarian and Ottoman Empires in the other. The Crown Heads of Europe were all related and all sought to preserve, and extend, their empires. When Archduke Franz Ferdinand of Austria was assassinated, the mobilisations and ultimatums began, and war broke out.

Britain hesitated until "tiny" Belgium was invaded by Germany as part of its thrust into France. When the Mayor of Bendigo read the proclamation of War from the Town Hall steps, people wildly cheered the expected news. An ethos of "Tally Ho – All For The War" exploded throughout the country.

At the outbreak of war, the Sultan of Turkey had called upon all Muslims in the British and French Empires to rise up in "Jihad" against Europeans. This was mostly ignored. Muslim leaders in India immediately reaffirmed their allegiance to Britain, as did the Muslims in Bendigo and elsewhere. The only time any attack ever took place in the Commonwealth was near Broken

Hill on New Year's Day 1915. Although described as being Turkish, two Afghani men opened fire on a train of civilian picnic goers, killing and injuring several. They were hunted down by the police and local residents and were both killed in the shootout that followed. Later that evening, angry residents of Broken Hill burnt the local German Club to the ground.

Enlistments from Bendigo were as strong as anywhere else as men rushed to join up. The Commonwealth Defence Act of 1909 had "exempted" those men who were not "substantially of European origin or descent" from combat roles, although they could be enlisted for other duties. In other words, only Europeans on the front lines please. In 1917, the rules were amended to allow a male to enlist if he had at least one European parent.

Members of the Bendigo Chinese community were eventually allowed to enlist, some already having been members of the Cadets and Citizens rifle clubs in the area. James Fooke, originally from the Bendigo area but living in Melbourne with his Tasmanian wife Margaret, was able to join the army in early 1916. Although his father was Chinese born, Fooke's mother was an Australian born European. After experiencing combat in both France and Belgium, Private James Fooke was killed at Passchendaele Ridge in October 1917. Other Chinese residents known to have enlisted include Frederick Foon, James Siakew and Albert Lagoon known as Lougoon.

What was known as "The Great War" was far more horrific and costly than anyone could imagine. From Gallipoli through to the final push in 1918, the bodies piled up on all sides due to the nationalistic pride in country, empire and what was regarded as a proper cause – shared by all combatants no matter which side they were on. Certainly "back home" things were not always good for those who had originally been born in what was now an enemy state.

From the beginning of the war, the Commonwealth Government took steps to monitor the activities of the still sizeable German population. All German nationals – even those who had been "naturalised" as British subjects – had to report to their local police stations regularly. Some metropolitan newspapers carried stories suggesting that as many as 3,000 Germans in the country were actually spies. William Vahland, who had been a British subject for half a century and an Anglican to boot, had to report to the Bendigo Police Station and inform authorities of his movements. At the grand old age of 86, this must have been an enormous insult to an old man who had given of his talents to create a majestic series of buildings in Bendigo and surrounding settlements. William Vahland would pass in May 1915, remembered by thousands as a great architect and officially regarded as an enemy alien.

In Ireland during Easter of 1916, a great uprising would occur that shook some of the foundations of the British Empire. The Irish Catholic Republican Group Sinn Fein, which is pronounced Shin Fane, Gaelic for "Ourselves, Alone", staged an armed rebellion against British rule. The British Army was swift to respond, even resorting to artillery to clear public buildings occupied by the militants. The response was savage, with surviving ringleaders arrested, quickly put to trial and executed by firing squad. Although this caused consternation far and wide, the Irish Hibernian Society in Melbourne was quick to denounce Sinn Fein and pledged continuing allegiance to Britain and the War Effort. The Bendigo St Patrick's Day parades would show great patriotic allegiance to Britain as well. However, there was some rumbling within the Greenest of the Irish community, and to the Orangemen this uprising validated their concerns about Catholicism, especially the Irish variety. Great concern was voiced towards the Archbishop, Dr Daniel Mannix, the Irish born head of the Catholic Church in Melbourne. Very Irish and very outspoken, Dr Mannix would be a mighty thorn in the side of what was to happen next.

For some of the war years, William Morris Hughes had been Prime Minister and Member for Bendigo in the Commonwealth Parliament. It is fair to say that in his long career, he was a Member for many other electorates as well, although not all at once! Hughes, London born and brought up Presbyterian, was very Protestant in his views on the Catholic faith. "Billy Hughes", as he was often called, served in nearly every political party of his day. Was he an opportunist? Simple answer: Yes. Known for his bad temper and fiery use of language, he gained almost a cult-like reputation, enabling him to win a seat wherever he stood as candidate. On visiting Australian troops in the trenches, he was dubbed "the Little Digger" - he wasn't overly tall by the way.

Worried by falling enlistments in 1916, the Government held a plebiscite, or poll, seeking to gain support for the conscription of eligible men into the military. The Catholic Church, under Dr Mannix, was vehemently opposed to conscription and the war itself. Hughes had organised a group calling itself the National Federation – very British and Protestant to the core. The 1916 plebiscite was a win for those against conscription. Never to be outdone, another vote was held in 1917 with a similar result. Hughes and his many supporters saw the results as being due to the actions of Mannix and seriously questioned the Irishman about his loyalty to the Empire.

Although sectarianism did play a part in the polls results, the full horrors of what the war entailed was brought home by the casualty lists posted on the notice boards of the Advertiser and the Independent. Films such as newsreels brought a living picture to what was happening overseas – although rarely showing images of deceased Allied soldiers. And the conflict seemed to go on and on without end.

Russia had experienced two revolutions in 1917, with the Tsar removed in the first and the Bolshevik Communists under Lenin taking power in the second. By October 1918, Germany was in a similar position and the Kaiser fled to the Netherlands, claiming what we would call political asylum, which was granted.

Just after midnight on the 12th of November 1918, an Armistice, or ceasefire was announced from the steps of the Bendigo Town Hall. The crowd joined hands and sung the hymn "Nearer My God To Thee" as the bells of St Paul's Cathedral peeled, along with the fire bell in View Street. The war had taken a terrible toll on every community and left quite significant sectarian tensions throughout the country. The royal heads of Germany, Russia and the former Austro-Hungarian empire were gone. Within a few years, the Sultanate would be abolished in Turkey by Mustafa Kemal, the Commander of the Dardanelles who saved his country from allied invasion.

Coming home was difficult for many soldiers, even those who had escaped physical injury. A very powerful type of influenza named the Spanish 'Flu, was bought back by the troops and claimed millions of lives around the world. Life as many had known it was changed forever. Most mines in Bendigo were now closed and one in Pall Mall was identified as the site for a Soldiers Memorial, this being the Hustler's Royal Reserve mine.

The British Empire had been victorious, which was something of a cold comfort for those women left without their husbands, brothers and sons. The war years had seen rapid developments in aviation and motor vehicles, which had become a more common sight. It was hoped that it would be the last war for all time. As the guns fell silent, many would have felt that life would go on as they had known it, but there would be great cultural changes and challenges to come.

CHAPTER THIRTEEN

THE ROARING 20'S AND 30'S INDEED

The war years had seen some advancement in the roles of women. Somewhat small in number, there was a beginning of the emancipation of women into what were regarded as strictly male domains. Bit by bit, women were enrolling in university studies, and emerging as lawyers and doctors and so forth. Even the Victorian Police started to employ women as Officers, although initially as "Auxiliaries". Many local women would find employment in such companies as the Hanro Knitting Mill, meaning a household could have two "breadwinners" and not the traditional single one which was male. The 1920's would see a big change in women's fashion – for the "Flapper", close fitting clothing would enhance the feminine shape, rather than trying to obscure it. The days of multi-layered dresses were gone, no doubt to the dismay of the more conservative older women.

Unfortunately, many of the old cultural divisions still remained and sectarianism in Bendigo would make the national press in mid-1920. The cause of this "scandal" was a play, written by a local Catholic priest, the Rev John Kennedy. No known copies of this play seem to exist today, but we are aware of its overall theme and the furore it produced.

Kennedy, who had authored a number of novels, wrote a play entitled "Advance Australia" – a play that questioned the true motives behind the war and how Australia had blindly rushed to join in, and the price that was paid for it. In modern terms we would call it an anti-war play. The Rev Kennedy had been a chaplain in France and had been awarded the Distinguished Service Order. The play was to be performed at the Royal Princess Theatre.

Kennedy's timing could not have been any worse. There was open conflict in Ireland by a number of Republican groups to win Irish independence. Archbishop Mannix, on his way to Britain and then America via Cork in Ireland on board the ship "The Baltic", found himself arrested by British military police who boarded the ship before it arrived in Cork. Mannix was forcibly removed and sent directly to Britain. Although the Melbourne based cleric had been opposed to the violent 1916 Easter uprising, he vocally supported the new, violent push for a free Ireland. As Mannix was on his way back to Australia, the Commonwealth Government unsuccessfully tried to bar his return. Locally and elsewhere, the still very loyal residents of the Empire were sensitive to criticism of the war, given the substantial toll it had taken on families and entire communities throughout the country. Add to that the seditious actions of Irish Catholics in Ireland and support amongst the same right here, it was inevitable that some loyal Britishers would be outraged. And they were.

The play to be performed at the Royal Princess Theatre in the first week of July 1920, caused a furore that made its way into the national press. The National Federation called for an Indignation Meeting to be held at the Bendigo Town Hall on July the 9th. All loyal Britishers were called to denounce the play, which was regarded as being seditious. The Irish Hibernian Associations denounced the Federation, as well as the Masons and Orange Lodges, who had denounced Kennedy and his play. As the meeting got underway, a small group of women and young men gathered across the road and sang "God Save Ireland" as a protest. Some youths climbed in through the Town Hall's side windows, obviously to disrupt the meeting, with a short scuffle ensuing before they were ejected.

A few nights later, Kennedy and his supporters held a large demonstration where Kennedy denied his play was seditious, rather it showed that it was the imperialism of both Britain and Germany that had dragged the country into war, and he was calling for a greater sense of a national Australian identity. I would suggest those comments probably didn't sway those who adhered to a culture of Empire.

In time, the play itself became history but in its wake were simmering sectarian divisions between Catholics and Protestants. The Irish would win a Free Irish State in December 1922. This state was granted Dominion status of the British Empire until 1937, when a completely independent Irish Republic came into being. The northern county of Ulster, which was staunchly Protestant, was, and still is, a part of the United Kingdom.

As part of what had happened during "The Great War", a new national public holiday was proclaimed in 1927. This was named ANZAC Day, a commemoration of the landing in April 1915 of Australian and New Zealand Army Corps at Gallipoli.

The 1920's were not as roaring in Bendigo as they appeared to be in other places. In fact, Bendigo's roaring days appeared to be over, rather lived in the previous century. With non-European immigration now effectively halted and immigration to Australia quite small, people could simply work and enjoy a British style of life with an overlay of a particular Australian flavour. Meat and three vegetables, roasted or fried, were the order of the day, with tea as the premier hot beverage. Beer was the most popular of the alcoholic beverages and the smoking of tobacco in pipes and cigars give way to cigarettes – which means "little cigar". The only take-away food, apart from sandwiches, were pies and pasties. Along with fish and chips. Very British indeed.

One non-British family of immigrants had found their way to Bendigo in early 1895 and established a business in Pall Mall in 1916 that became a favourite until it closed in 1973. The Favoloro brothers were Italian and their business was able to seat up to 150 patrons. We might think that they might have served up pizza, ravioli or a risotto, but that was not the case, probably due to the British tastes of the local population. The brothers served up three course meals, light lunches and the like. Outside on the footpath, cakes, scones, buns and tarts were sold from a stall. It was probably too early to tempt locals with a taste of Italy, especially with a generous amount of garlic.

The introduction of the Basic Wage in 1907 had given working people greater income so as to enjoy life more fully. This was a world first by the way. Shortages of labour during the war had increased prices of nearly everything, so the 1920's were a time of reasonable living for most people. The pictures theatres of Bendigo did a roaring trade, even more so with the introduction of sound to film in the late 1920's. These were the "Talkies" and the influence of American culture began to take hold. Hollywood reigned supreme as the world's movie making capital and locals became accustomed to American slang, along with stories about gangsters, the Wild West, American history and humour in general. Incidentally, America had outlawed alcohol in 1918, which was a major victory for the Temperance Movement there, giving hope to the local societies but little else. From 1918 until the repeal of Prohibition in 1933, the "Great Experiment" spawned vast criminal empires and all sorts of damaging bootleg alcohol and should have been dubbed the "Great Dismal Failure".

Australian Arts, that is literature, film, plays and art floundered during this time. Australian films found it difficult to get screenings, although many that did attract reasonable audiences. The "best" of the arts always appeared to hail from overseas, such was the preference for foreign product.

When the Wall Street Stock Exchange crashed in 1929, the world spun into a great economic depression. Unemployment rose to a point in Australia with one third thrown out of work. The Victorian Government inaugurated a scheme whereby unemployed men would be given an allowance to look for gold. Gold mining centres like Bendigo experienced a newer, although less feverish, return to prospecting. Times were hard and the imported, now readily available "underground mutton", that is the rabbit, became a staple meat source for many families.

Sports became a focal point for people trying to escape what was now a very difficult time. Bendigonians followed the "Bodyline" cricket series and cheered on a new national hero, Don Bradman. A few years earlier, the Victorian Football Association had undergone a split, with a Victorian Football League being established in Melbourne. New heroes all brought closer to home with new technology and a new Government Commission -the Australian Broadcasting Commission. Radio arrived and those able to afford it could listen to news, sports and entertainment programs, revolutionising communication. Record players were becoming more common and electricity was being connected to more homes and businesses.

A new public holiday was added to the Victorian calendar in 1931. This was called Australia Day, to commemorate the arrival of the British in January 1788. It should be noted that the public holiday was not always celebrated on the 26th of January, as quite often it was held on the nearest Monday so that people could enjoy a long weekend. In Sydney, First Nation people began to demonstrate on the day, seeing it as an invasion day instead.

As the difficult years of the 1930's wore on, Bendigonians lived in an overall Anglo-Saxon Celtic cocoon, with some prodding via Hollywood. The dwindling Chinese population still sourced Chinese participants for the Easter Procession, with the "Hindoos" and other ethnic minorities slowly making their way to the cemeteries. The Dja Dja Wurrung people were few and widely flung from Bendigo – an oasis of Anglo-Australiana. In Germany, Italy and Japan, a militaristic nationalism was rising to a crescendo, ultimately crashing down upon the residents of Bendigo and leading to an inevitable change in the way Australia would see itself in the world.

CHAPTER FOURTEEN

THE EMPIRE'S LAST HARRAH

The year 1939 had begun with record heat, drought and the massive Black Friday bushfires leaving over 70 people dead. Bendigo had seen a new gold mine open that year, right on High Street, the Central Deborah Mine. Here and there, dotted around the suburban streets were the Californian Bungalow styles of housing, along with the curvaceous signature of Art Deco architecture. Although there had been a drop in tensions in Europe during 1938, with British Prime Minister Neville Chamberlain getting a written guarantee from German Chancellor Adolf Hitler promising "peace in our time", by winter things looked grim indeed.

With the German invasion of Poland on 1st September 1939, the residents of Bendigo awaited another expected announcement – Britain declared war on the 3rd and Australian Prime Minister Robert Menzies announced that Australia was also at war. The crowds did not cheer this time – sons and daughters of the Great War veterans found themselves facing the German and Italians and a very uncertain future. For German and Italian residents throughout the country, their future lay in internment camps, being made prisoners until the war's end.

The fall of Western Europe to the Nazi Germans was swift, followed by the Battle of Britain which almost saw Britain experience invasion as well. Australian troops and nurses found themselves in the Middle East, with some Australian pilots being posted to Britain itself. Women were recruited to new positions in the military for the first time – as administrators in the

Army and Navy and ground crew in the Air Force and in Civil Defence positions. Due to so many men leaving farms, women were recruited into a new Land Army. In time women found employment with the Bendigo Tramways as conductors – all of this a radical change in the culture of the roles of women in society.

With the Japanese attack on the U.S. Navy at Pearl Harbour in December 1941 and the massive invasions throughout Indo-China and the Pacific, it was generally feared that the Japanese could very well invade Australia as well. The fear of being swamped by Asians appeared to be an appalling reality – the Japanese soldiers were known for their savage treatment of conquered people, Asian and European. From December of that year, Bendigo's homes had blacked out windows – the lights could be seen from the air and might indicate targets to Japanese aircraft. All street sings were removed and the street themselves blacked out at night.

In early 1942, American soldiers were billeted to Bendigo, although for a short time. The new Australian Prime Minister, John Curtin, made a speech that would redefine Australia's links to Britain and the United States – Australian would now look to America. The British colony of Singapore, 'Fortress Singapore', had easily fallen to the Japanese, with tens of thousands of Australian and British troops becoming prisoners. Britain was incapable of protecting its far-flung empire, although most locals still had a fondness for it.

The Second World War, although victorious for the Allies, would signal an end to the British, French and Dutch Empires, especially in the Asian – Pacific region, with America becoming a powerful military and cultural presence in the area, which still stands today. The multiple Japanese air raids on Darwin, Broome and Port Hedland, as well as midget submarine attacks in Sydney Harbour, made it clear that Australia could not defend itself. Too big a country with too small a population – around eight million in 1940. There would have to be a cultural shift in this country's approach to immigration. The days of being an outpost of Britain were now definitely over for all time.

CHAPTER FIFTEEN

THE DOOR CREAKS OPEN.

John Curtin died in office before the war's end and he was replaced by Ben Chifley – well known for having been a train driver before entering Parliament. The Minister for Immigration was Victorian Arthur Caldwell, also well known for his ability to speak "straight from the shoulder", "without mincing his words". A 1943 poll had shown that 90% of Australians wanted an increase in immigration after the war. Of that 90%, 40% actually wanted unlimited immigration. In September of 1944, a Post - War Immigration Committee found that although British migration was favoured, it would be insufficient to meet new immigration goals. The target for British immigrants would be 70,000 per year, with an incentive scheme whereby immigrants would pay 10 pounds towards the ship's fare, the rest would be paid by the Commonwealth.

In 1947, faced with a shortage of both shipping and willing British migrants, Caldwell visited a displaced persons camp in Germany. Keep in mind that displaced persons after the war numbered 20 million. The Commonwealth Government signed an agreement with the International Refugee Organisation and the first of many refugees from the Baltic States, Scandinavia and Eastern Europe began to arrive in capital cities. The Australian Council of Trade Unions, the Returned Servicemen's League and many Municipal Councils were strongly opposed to the idea. For the ACTU, it was a question about jobs being taken from Australian workers. For the RSL, it was a question about whose side these immigrants were on during the war. For the Councils, it was both of those reasons, plus what it would do to the British fabric of their local areas – the immigrants were foreigners after all. Caldwell came up with a term to describe these non-British arrivals. They were called "New Australians", a term that would last for around 30 years to describe any European national.

The Displaced Persons Programme ran from 1947 to 1952, when it was abolished. It would see 170,000 people arrive who were "indented" to the Government for two years. They were meant to "assimilate' quickly in Australian society and to help, English language classes were held on the migrant ships enroute. Very few of these people ever made their way to Bendigo, although I do know of a Lithuanian man, Paul Vaitkus, who came here in the mid-1950's and married a local girl. Their son Ron is still a local resident.

From 1948, alongside British migrants, Australia attracted massive numbers of Greeks and Italians. Notably, Italy had sided with Germany during the war, but surely it is amazing that there was very little animosity from either Anglo or Italian "New Australians" as they began to mix. Once again, Bendigo did poorly from this massive wave of immigration. Shepparton, on the other hand, received large numbers of Italians, probably to work in the orchards. Many Italians would go on to buy their own orchards, increasing fruit production substantially.

Bendigo did receive a number of Dutch migrants in the mid 1950's, all bused up from a migrant hostel in Daylesford. Speaking to one of our Dutch community, who was 14 at the time of her arrival in Bendigo, I was told that the reception they got was somewhat "frosty" – the migrants seen as a threat to the jobs that locals might otherwise get. Bendigo historian, Mr James Lerk, arrived in Bendigo as a boy via New South Wales and upon walking into a shop with his mother, the female shopkeeper greeted them with "Oh, so you're the foreigners", as if a strange rumour about the Dutch had suddenly been proved real.

As you are probably aware, the post war immigration wave was solidly European, however, in 1949, 800 non-European and Japanese War Brides of Australian military personnel were allowed to settle. Robert Menzies was back as Prime Minister at this time. The Japanese were largely detested due to the war time atrocities committed by their soldiers, so certainly the Japanese women and their husbands may have had a very difficult time.

By 1961, 9% of the Australian population was now non-British with a greater percentage of Australian born having a parent born in a non-English speaking country. An old British word for Indians now spread throughout the continent to describe the Italian and Greek people – "wogs". The term also applied if someone was unwell, they had "the wog". In time, especially in nearby Melbourne, the Australian born children of the European migrants would wear the name "wog" with pride – a strange twist if ever there was one, but coming from Melbourne, I know this was the case. For your edification, let me assure you that when I went to Thornbury High School, I could swear in five languages.

The White Australia Policy, implemented in 1901, took a mighty fall when the Dictation Test was officially abolished in 1958. It could no longer stand in the face of this wave of immigration. The 1966 Migration Act saw increased non-European immigration, a bit of an after-thought of the 1950 Colombo Plan, that enabled young Asian people the opportunity to study in Australia. In 1966, a trickle of Vietnamese refugees were allowed to settle in Australia, as the Vietnam War raged on. Amongst the earliest of the mid 1960's non-European immigrants were from member countries of the British Commonwealth of Nations, namely India and Malaysia.

By the mid 1960's, the Immigration Restriction Act of 1901 had effectively become null and void. The 1960's, as a decade, was a time of quite revolutionary upheaval, especially in Western style democracies. Traditional values, institutions and paradigms came under serious question from an emerging youth culture. The massive global birth rate which increased immediately following World War Two, has probably been the single biggest rise in population ever recorded. This post-war generation was aptly given the title "Baby Boomers" and the 1960's saw the oldest of them starting to achieve adulthood. The wave of post war immigration into Australia would change the country forever. Bendigo, unlike many other major urban areas, did not receive a massive influx of non-British people, creating an almost island effect of Anglo-Australiana culture. This would have ramifications in the decades to come.

CHAPTER SIXTEEN

ISLAND IN THE SUN

After 1945, Bendigo seemed to continue in a business as usual sort of way. The official flag of the country was still the Union Jack of Britain, with the Red Ensign being used as a close second. The Red Ensign had the Union Jack in the top left-hand corner of the flag, with a large six pointed stars underneath representing the six States. Both the Australian Capital Territory and the Northern Territory are not officially states, so they are not included. On the right of the flag, the stars of the Southern Cross appear. The Flag itself is a dull red colour. It was the flag of the Australian Infantry Force in both World Wars. This would change in 1954 at the behest of the Commonwealth Government under Robert Menzies. It was the Cold War – the West versus the Communist states of the Soviet Union and China, with red being a communist's colour of choice! The Blue Ensign replaced the dull red one and is now the official flag of Australia. The change in ensigns did cause a bit of a stir amongst imperialists.

From the end of the war, American cultural dominance continued largely through films, music, fashion and food. Women wore dresses that would cover their knees, with a "slip' underneath. Something called Jeans, pants made from denim, became more common. Although the Big Band sounds had been popular during the war years, the 1950's gave way to Rock and Roll – faster, small group music with lyrics, all based on the Rhythm and Blues of the Afro-American culture. Hamburgers started to appear on the menus at fish and chip shops, with instant coffee starting to make inroads as well. The Temperance Societies, the Orange Lodges and the like faced rapidly declining membership as younger people now felt no need to join these old "straight-laced" groups. The times were a changing.

Church attendances had been good until after 1945, when a slow decline in numbers became apparent. Many returned servicemen turned their backs on religion with an increasing number of young people seeing little relevance in it at all. Over the rest of the century, many Bendigo churches would close, especially of the Methodist variety. It would seem that the Boomers did not share the abstinent views of that church, and they wanted to dance. Ultimately, the Uniting Church would be born, mostly an amalgamation of Methodist and Presbyterian churches, although not all.

Despite an apparent overlay of Americana influence, most Bendigonians still had a great love for British royalty. When the Alexandra Fountain was opened on the 5th of July 1881 by Princes Albert and George, people turned out in their thousands. With every pun intended, the crowning glory came on 5 March 1954, when Queen Elizabeth II and Prince Phillip arrived in Bendigo by train. This was the first time a reigning monarch had visited Bendigo, albeit for a few hours as part of the tour of the British Commonwealth. The Upper Reserve, soon to be renamed the Queen Elizabeth Oval, saw around 9,000 school children and 50,000 adults greet the royal couple, who rode around the oval in a Land Rover. It was nowhere near a cold day either!

So, Bendigo sailed on – one foot still infatuated with royalty, the other dipping a few toes into a new, burgeoning American world culture. A Bendigo television station opened in 1961, bringing the world a bit closer to home on the relatively small sized screens – all in living black and white.

European migration to Bendigo was small, although when Italian stone masons were brought out to work on the Sacred Heart Cathedral, they bought their families with them. Many of the wives were employed in a factory which produced a new fabric named Lycra. And speaking of fashion, when English model Jean Shrimpton wore a "mini-skirt" revealing her knees, without a hat, at the 1964 Melbourne Cup, it made news worldwide. The mini-skirt, along with the bikini, would become synonymous with a social and cultural change by young people in the 1960's. Those fashions, which would have ended in a young lady's arrest once upon a time, still have great popularity today. Men's fashion became more relaxed and colourful being influenced by the rising "Hippy" culture from the United States. The wearing of hats belonged to the older generation and the rather distinctive smell of cannabis started to waft out of windows here and there.

For a time, Bendigo youth danced to the music of British based bands such as the Beatles and the Rolling Stones. Even the Americans took to the new style of rock and roll, or "pop" music as it was being called. Then came the American Jefferson Airplane, Janis Joplin, Jimi Hendrix, just to name a few. There was Billy Thorpe who, as a kid, was a "ten-pound tourist" from the United Kingdom.

The Vietnam war raged, and conscription forced young men into the military, or face two years imprisonment. Social unrest amongst generations developed, as some young people began to rebel against authority, while those of the war years, especially ex-servicemen, supported the war and conscription. Whereas earlier youthful generations had done what their elders had told them to do, many young people openly defied those expectations.

The 1960's and 1970's saw a huge shift in cultural perspectives, actively propelled by the Baby Boomers who wanted and welcomed change.

In May of 1967, a referendum that sought to give the Aboriginal people of Australia full citizenship by way of counting them in the census, was massively successful. The referendum also transferred Aboriginal Affairs from the States to the Commonwealth. This was a major turning point in First Nation/Non First Nation relations, with Aboriginal people finally being "granted" recognition for being human, just like everyone else. That same year, the Australian and Turkish governments signed an agreement allowing Turks to migrate to Australia, permitting Muslim people to take up permanent residence.

In what I consider to be a bit odd, all throughout the years 1901 to 1975, all British subjects had the right to vote, even if they had arrived two months before any election. Some of the British found it a bit odd too, as they really didn't know who to vote for or what the issues were. Until 1948, when Australia developed its own citizenship process, any other national could take out British Naturalization and become a British subject. The move from being born in Bendigo as a British subject in 1947, to be born an Australian citizen in 1949 was quite a major point of differentiation.

As the 1970's began, the Boomers, and the older generation who wanted change, elected the Government of Gough Whitlam. A new type of national identity was being formed, a country of migrants, forged into one, acknowledging the traditional owners of country. Speaking about the end of the White Australia Policy, Immigration Minister Al Grassby famously said: "Give me a shovel and I'll bury it" and that is what he did. Bendigo was still an island of Anglo-Australianhood, with small numbers of migrants making their way to Bendigo over the last decades of the century. This could not last, as the rest of the world started to arrive much as it did in the 1850's. To some Bendigonians, a multicultural society seemed more than inviting. To others, the appearance of people a bit different to themselves caused anxiety, tension and outright hostility.

CHAPTER SEVENTEEN

PIZZA WITH THE LOT.

E arly on in the research for this book, I wondered when did the first pizza make its appearance in Bendigo. The formation of a Bendigo Caledonian Society in the 1850's gives us a date for the Haggis, but what about the iconic Italian masterpiece?

Bendigo Historical Society member, Carol Evans, remembers a café in McCrae Street run by an Italian man named Fred, which was probably a short form of Frederico. As part of the menu, pizza was available. It was a long time ago and Coral does not remember the exact year, although probably sometime in the early 1960's. Food can be a great bridge in cultural acceptance and understanding, although it can be a slow process depending on the individual or family concerned. I had my first pizza in 1979, at the age of 22, although not because there was a shortage of pizza shops at the time. Bendigonians took to pizzas much the same as elsewhere around the country and also experienced expresso coffee - Italians imported their beloved machines as soon as businesses opened up, for they enjoyed real coffee, just like the Greeks and other continental Europeans.

Two of the earliest pizza shops were Clogs, which was opened in 1974 by three Dutch brothers, John, Frank and Martin Van Haandel, as well as the nearby Belvedere. Clogs still exists in the original premises in Pall Mall, in a building designed by William Vahland in 1860. The pizza rush was underway and still continues its dominance.

The original Chinese residents had their own eating places since the 1850's, although it would appear the European residents didn't take to Chinese food for quite some time. In 1892, Peter Louey Mow started the Toi Shan café in Mitchell Street, which is the oldest Chinese food establishment in Bendigo and certainly one of the oldest in the country. The earliest forms of Chinese takeaway saw customers bringing their own saucepans or other containers to collect the cooked food, which they would reheat when they got back home.

Because of massive immigration from Europe and then the rest of the world, Melbourne developed a reputation for global cuisine, as well as "fusion", which is mixing cultural foods and serving them up on one plate. The large number of Vietnamese refugees, following the conquest of South Vietnam in 1975 and other refugees and migrants from South East Asia, really added to the blend of food choices. Despite over 300,000 Vietnamese arrivals in the 1970's and early 1980's, very few Bendigo residents are Vietnamese or first generation Australian born. Most would stay in the capital cities, revitalising old shopping strips and turning Chinese New Year into Asian New Year. Likewise, Turkish immigration and refugees from Lebanon would continue to add to the cultural mix of the city. Once again, during the final three decades of the last century, only a trickle of new immigrants or refugees made their way up the Calder. In many ways this has been the result of State and Commonwealth policy – migrants are brought into capital cities where resources to re-settle them are far more concentrated. Once settled, various national/cultural groupings tend to gravitate together for mutual support. This was very much what happened on the goldfields back in the 1850's and 1860's, so it is a human thing rather than a perceived cultural requirement.

With worldwide migration across the globe escalating from the 1990's – some of it via regular immigration, the rest from waves of refugees fleeing conflict, famine and natural occurrences such as flooding and environmental considerations, Australia was opening its door to a new wave of people seeking safety or a better life for themselves and their children. It was inevitable that many migrants and refugees from around the world would start arriving in Bendigo, and initially there was a genuine, bi-partisan political approach to it all. By the dawn of the new 21st century, Melbourne was home to a variety of multicultural festivals: the very Greek Glendi; a Spanish Festival; Asian New Year; as well as Moomba. Most people got along quite well and sampling another's culture in its myriad of forms became commonplace. For a time, as representatives from around the world began to make Bendigo home, all appeared to be very well.

The movement for full recognition of First Nation people and their culture continued to gain momentum in the 1960's, 1970's and 1980's. What is known as NAIDOC Week stems from the Day of Mourning held in Sydney on Australian Day in 1938. The National Aborigines and Islanders Day Committee was formed with the observance day moved to July in 1957. Held nationally form 1972, this week celebrates First Nation Culture in its diversity and richness, as well as highlighting ongoing concerns regarding sovereignty, equality and ending all discrimination.

The 1980's saw most First Nation Australians form incorporated association to further these aims. Locally, the Dja Dja Wurrung Clans Corporation was established, and it has achieved some great initiatives over the past 30 years. One such success involved the Jaara Baby, re-discovered in storage at the Museum Victoria in 1994. This baby, wrapped in a possum skin bundle and hidden in a tree hollow near Charlton, was found by a wood cutter in 1904. The bundle also contained traditional and European artefacts, suggesting the time of death and internment was between the 1840's and 1860's. It might have been the child of an elder or chief. For 90 years it had been in storage, long forgotten. After a long legal battle, the Jaara Baby was returned to Country on the 10th of September 2003, with a handover ceremony including traditional dances by Dja Dja Wurrung and Wurundjeri people. The Jaara Baby, in its original bundle, was then reburied. That it took so long to return the remains indicates there is still a long road to travel for full, inclusive reconciliation.

In 1992, the Mabo Decision of the High Court overturned the doctrine of Terra Nullius (empty land), thereby re-establishing that Indigenous Land Rights still existed. This decision is still being played out, even locally, as traditional owners get greater participation in land management practices and the preservation of cultural sites.

And we should not forget the deliberate policies of both Federal and State governments that led to what is known as the Stolen Generations. From 1905 through to 1967, when the First Australians finally had the official status of people to be counted in the census, a policy of assimilating Aboriginal people into white society was implemented. Put simply, the Aboriginals were to have their Aboriginality removed from them. This was conducted by a vigorous policy of removing children from their parents by force. The children were placed into white foster care and orphanages and brought up strictly in a European way. The final vestiges of this policy of cultural cleansing were not fully extinguished until early in the 1970's. Official statistics vary as to what percentage of children were forcibly removed, but at least one in three to one in ten were subject to this vicious policy. The heartache and trauma is something that is still to be fully reckoned with.

As calls for an apology from the Federal government grew in the 1990's and early 2000's, then Prime Minister John Howard stalled. Massive rallies across the nation in the year 2000 still went unheeded. Following the election of a new government in 2007, Prime Minister Kevin Rudd delivered The Apology speech in Parliament on the 13th of February 2008. A true healing and reconciliation was then able to commence. Much of the push for this official recognition of a vicious policy and the enormous suffering that followed, was due to the work of the First Nation People themselves, fully supported by those in the European generations who wanted to see big societal change and justice. Many of the more recent "rest of the world" arrivals also wanted to see a society that recognised the first inhabitants of "the wide brown land".

At this point, considering that a large number of global citizens were arriving in this country, we turn our attention to the establishment of a place of worship that helps put Bendigo on a global footing. This great Buddhist temple, or Stupa, really sets the stage for Bendigo to become an inland centre of multifaith practice and dialogue – and dialogue between faiths really has its own imperative at this point in human history.

The origins of The Great Stupa of Universal Compassion goes back to 1971, when Melbourne based advertising man, Ian Green, went on a trip to India. Somewhat disaffected with the materialistic, consumerist world, Ian

Green found a rejuvenation in Buddhist principles. In 1981, following an inheritance of a large parcel of land at Myer's Flat, Ian and his partner Judy, also a Buddhist, along with their children lived on the land in an old railway carriage. In time, they established the Atisha Centre as a place for meditation, retreats and Buddhist celebrations with their friends.

The Great Stupa of Universal Compassion

When Lama Thubten Yeshe of the Mahayana Tradition visited the site, he thought that a Stupa should be constructed, enabling the surrounding land to become a place of Buddhist practice, including a monastery. This would be a huge and expensive undertaking, made even more so when Lama Zopa Rinpoche had a vision to model the Stupa on the great Stupa of Gyantse in Tibet. Almost 50 metres high and 50 metres square at its base, this would be the biggest Stupa in the Southern Hemisphere. The expected cost was put at $20 million, which had to be raised via donations. Even more outstanding was the discovery in Canada of a massive 18 tonne boulder of gem quality jade, perfect for a statue of the Buddha to be sculptured from. Named "The Polar Pride", the Greens set about raising $1 million to buy it in 2003. The donations were forthcoming, with the Jade Buddha for Universal Peace being made a reality.

The Stupa was intended to be a place of multi-faith worship, so the plans included areas for non-Buddhist traditions as well as other Buddhist paths. The Stupa, therefore, was to be a centre to promote peace and harmony in the world, despite any theological differences.

In June 2007, His Holiness the Dalai Lama arrived at the site to bless the Great Stupa. The Bendigo region had never before experienced the visitation of the head of a major world religion, but as the Dalai Lama likes to say: "I'm just a simple Buddhist monk", meaning we can all make some spiritual progress if we choose and that was what he was seeking to do himself.

In 2009, the Jade Buddha began to travel around the world, with donations from its exhibition helping to finance the cost of the Stupa. Every May, the celebration of the birth of the Buddha – Visak – was held on an ever-increasing scale at Myer's Flat. Earning the title "Festival of Light", thousands of people would attend the events which saw performances of Jaara people, Chinese lion dancers, fire dancers plus fireworks. Very much a labour of love, the Great Stupa of Universal Compassion stands high above the trees and serves as a reminder that we are one humanity, with great diversity within that humanity.

As much as the Restricted Immigration Act of 1901 had intended to preserve a fully European nation, there were some cracks in this almost impenetrable wall via the Certificate of Exemption from the Dictation Test. One such exemption was given to a Japanese family named Takasuka in 1914. The Commonwealth thought that it was appropriate for the country to have a rice industry, with the Takasuka's being "imported" to help in its establishment. Along with a number of rice varieties, a very young Soh Takasuka accompanied his parents. Calrose rice was the most successful of the rice varieties tried in southern New South Wales and a new industry was borne from Japanese expertise. Unfortunately for Soh, the war years saw him interned as an enemy alien. After the war, with Australian citizenship, the tomato grower and keen field naturalist entered local government in the Shire of Huntly. Soh Takasuka was President of the Shire from 1966 to 1970. Although animosity towards the Japanese was still high amongst those of the older generations, certainly there were enough voters in Huntly who put the old animosity behind them to vote for Takasuka.

Although the number of Chinese in Bendigo certainly waned, Chinese culture was still a noted feature in Bendigo. In 1970, the original imperial Dragon, Loong, was replaced with Sun Loong, which means "new dragon". Just as Bendigonians had a traditional attachment to Loong, Sun Loong quickly attracted that same affection. The Easter procession would not be the same without a mighty dragon. The Bendigo Trust opened the Dai Gum San (Big Gold Mountain) Wax Works in the old Temperance Hall in View Street in 1975. The 60 wax figures were originally made in Hong Kong by Vivian Sun in 1973 for local display. Being given to the Bendigo Trust, these wax figures gave Bendigo an extra insight into southern Chinese culture. When the waxworks closed in the late 1980's, care of the figures was given to the Bendigo Chinese Association.

By the 1980's, much of the old Chinatown in Bendigo had been demolished and an increasing number of artefacts were being held in storage. Russell Jack proposed a purpose-built museum to display the history of the Chinese, not just in Bendigo, but throughout the country. Fundraising began in 1988 and in 1991 the Golden Dragon Museum was officially opened. Housing Loong, Sun Loong and a myriad of Chinese artefacts with an increasing number of donated items, the Museum is currently looking to expand its premises to showcase the many valuable items that remain in storage. The Dai Gum San Precinct, with its plaza, Imperial Gardens and Temple, has become not just a major tourist and research centre, but also a place to gather for Chinese New Year and Harvest Moons festivals. The biggest crowds assemble at Easter for the "Awakening of the Dragon" ceremony and at the procession's end when the dragon is led tail first back into the museum for another year.

Certainly, an increasing number of people from around the world are deciding to make Bendigo home. To help in that settlement process, which can be quite lengthy depending on the needs of each individual or family, local agencies have arisen to meet that very personal need. The Loddon Campaspe Multicultural Service (LCMS) was first established in 1999 as the Bendigo Regional Ethnic Communities Council Inc. This agency provides support for newly arrived immigrants and refugees in the way of English programmes, employment, driver training, playgroup and the celebration of diversity through an annual Multicultural Festival, the first of which began in 2001. In 2013, this festival became a week-long event including an interfaith dinner, cultural workshops and a multicultural family day of entertainment, displays and international food. Bendigo Community Health Services also runs similar programmes, all designed to help new arrivals become accustomed to a new way of life and to help people achieve their full potential.

However, not all of Bendigo residents have felt comfortable with this big shift in the cultural demographic. Indeed, elsewhere there have been concerns as Australia opened its doors to the rest of the world. Certainly nothing would shake the foundations of Bendigo more than a desire of the local multinational Muslim community to build a place of worship. That simple and quite human need would seemingly propel Bendigo back to the 1850's, when a powerful movement against the Chinese seized the mentality of so many. The cause for religious freedom and a fair go for all was suddenly put to the test.

CHAPTER EIGHTEEN

IT DON'T COME EASY

Currently, nearly 50% of Australia's population was born overseas or have parents who were born overseas. With a population of 25 million people, that indicates that not only is Australia a very multicultural country, but it works extremely well given the high level of social cohesion. Bendigo, on the other hand, with decades of being predominantly an Anglo society, has only experienced rapid migration arrivals in the last decade or so. The 2011 Census showed that Bendigo had only 7% of its population being borne overseas, making it the least multicultural municipality of its size in the country. What appears next comes from the pages of the Bendigo Advertiser and Bendigo Weekly: the Melbourne Age; my own notes and recollection from the first two anti-mosque rallies, and the fabulous book by John Saffron: "Depends What You Mean By Extremist", published by Penguin/Hamish Hamilton in 2017.

In early 2014, the Bendigo Islamic Association purchased timbered land in Rowena Street, East Bendigo and submitted plans for a mosque to the council. With the approval of the Planning Department, the proposal was set to be heard by the councillors at the regular meeting on June 18. The councillors at this time were Rod Fyffe, Elise Chapman, Peter Cox, Lisa Ruffell, Rod Campbell, Helen Leach, Mark Weragoda and Barry Lyons who was Mayor. In the proceeding months, anti-Mosque opponents became very active in Bendigo. Battle lines were being drawn, with absolutely no help from events unfolding overseas.

From the attacks in America in 2001, there was a steady worldwide increase in extremist activities, even more so with the invasion of Iraq in 2003. The "Arab Spring" of 2011 saw the despotic government of Egypt fall, with a shocking civil war raging in Syria which continues. From that Syrian conflict, a group known as Daesh unleased an offensive from Syria into Northern Iraq and donned a term used in Western media as the "Islamic State". Known for its cruel and psychopathic terror tactics, even upon fellow Sunni Muslims as well as Shia Muslims, the I.S. called for attacks worldwide. Certainly, some very extreme attacks did occur in Europe. The Lindt Café Siege in Sydney could be cited as an attack, even though the perpetrator had only claimed to have become Sunni just days before the siege – having been a life-long Shia Muslim. Most Muslims worldwide were as appalled as anyone else. These groups, using Islam as a kind of excuse, really had political agendas to follow, each claiming to be the "true followers" of Islam.

So where did the anti-mosque actions spring from? In a lengthy article in the Advertiser, published on Saturday, 20th June 2014, a reprint of an Age article by Chris Johnston, the various networks of "far-right wing" politics was mapped out. A Queensland group called "Restore Australia", headed by two former Vietnam veterans, had a strong anti-Islamic agenda and had funded two groups opposed to the Bendigo mosque. The influence of social media should be noted, the Stop the Mosque in Bendigo Facebook page has a link to "Restore Australia". A number of small groups, including what was called the United Patriots Front (UPF), were all interconnected. The article also mentions a group hailing from the small coastal town of Wyee, just south of Newcastle NSW, who call themselves "Concerned Citizens". It was this group, obviously with local support who letter boxed my area with a small leaflet entitled "ISLAM THE FACTS". This leaflet was a tirade against Islam and multiculturalism in general and made the rather odd suggestion that Anglo-Australian couples should have lots of children – outbreed these Muslims was the point being made. I suspect it was modelled on an American tract, as the last pages includes the word penitentiary, which American use to describe what we usually refer to as gaols or prisons. This non-Shakespearean piece of literature ended with Christian undertones. There were other right wing political/religious groups involved as well, including

"Reclaim Australia" and "Rise Up Australia". The "Q Society" also had a part to play in all of this. In effect, these groups were what we might call mosque chasers, as they brought their forces together wherever a proposal to build a mosque or Islamic School happened to be. In many ways this has been a part of a rise in right wing, nationalist "patriotic" movements throughout the Western world. Chillingly, it is similar to movements once seen in the 1920's and 1930's, and we know what happened as a result of that.

Prior to the council meeting in June 2014, Cr Mark Weragoda had had his property decked out in black balloons by persons unknown. The councillor had also received threatening correspondence and at the meeting was racially abused. Around 250 people had attended the meeting, extraordinary actually, most to oppose the mosque. It was reported that a bus full of anti-mosque people had come up from Melbourne. The obviously ill-informed objectors failed to realise some basic truths about Mr Weragoda: he is an Australian citizen, born in Sri Lanka, whose father was an Anglican Minister at Maldon. He was regarded as being Islamic by the objectors, no doubt because of his deeper brown skin colour. Absolutely no point in letting facts get in the way of a "good story", a hallmark of these clearly racist groups.

At the meeting, police kept watch over the rowdy crowd and there was considerable uproar when the proposal to build a mosque was carried, five for and two against. Councillors Elsie Chapman and Helen Leech were against the mosque proposal. Just over 400 written objections had been received by Council, with many coming from Melbourne and interstate, mostly citing concerns about Islam itself rather than any planning issues. One local objection claimed, "That the horses are worried". Please don't ask me to analyse that one!

In the Bendigo Weekly's Editorial of Friday June 20th, 2014, the pro-mosque and multiculturalism paper wrote: "Yes, the Koran has some ugly elements. So does the Bible. Read Leviticus or Exodus if you want to make Christianity look bad or irrelevant". The Advertiser wrote editorials in a similar vein.

Opposition to the mosque increased as the objectors began to organise protests and a legal challenge in the Victorian Civil Administrative Tribunal (VCAT). Local resident, Julie Hoskin, became the leading figure in the legal action. Most of the mainstream Christian Churches backed the decision to build a mosque, along with a number of local organisations as well. Mr Heri Febriyanto was the spokesperson for the Bendigo Islamic Association and it fell to him to try and explain what Islam and a mosque were really about. The Jakarta born Australian citizen and IT consultant had long favoured and forged links with other religious faiths and social organisations. An early surprise and partnership came in the form of the "This is Bendigo" movement, brainchild of Haven-Home Safe CEO Ken Marchingo. Posters and car stickers with the logo, coupled with a lot of coloured balloons, began to appear in shops, offices and on cars. People who supported a multicultural Bendigo were encouraged to display coloured balloons outside their homes, a direct contrast to the infamous and nasty black balloons. Even the Anglican Cathedral and its statue of Captain Cook suddenly became ballooned.

In July 2014, a further local campaign got underway. This was "Racism. It Stops With Me", which also appeared on social media. At the same time, a truck with a large "Stop the Mosque" poster drove around the streets, as well as playing the Muslim call to prayer. A man was seen reading quotes from the Qur'an – perhaps he should have quoted Leviticus and Exodus as well. People from the parked truck at Lansell Square were seen to be handing out leaflets. And so, it went on.

On Saturday 19th of July 2014, a "This is Bendigo" rally was held in the Hargreaves Mall, with around 300 attending with lots of coloured balloons. The amiable Mayor, Barry Lyons, presided and led the crowd in a pledge: "Racisms, It stops with me", a campaign from the Australian Human Rights Commission. As an objection to the Council's decision went to VCAT, only the very hopeful would have thought that things would go quiet for a while.

The year 2015 would be like no other as far as Bendigo was concerned. The new Mayor, Peter Cox, was resolute and determined to do the right thing for all concerned. As the VCAT hearing against the mosque continued, Mayor Cox was quick to remind people that religious observance was guaranteed under Section 116 of the Commonwealth Constitution and that in a democratic society respect for other people's beliefs is not negotiable.

At the hearing, opposition to the mosque was initially based on planning issues such as traffic, parking and noise. This would degenerate into negative commentary about Islam – not helped by extremists overseas. The legal costs were escalating as Council had to mount a defence of its decision.

In Thursday, 6th August 2015, VCAT released its findings which overturned the objections to the mosque, giving it the go ahead. Mayor Cox stated: "The independent umpire has given their decision, and I am hoping that people will respect and accept that". Unfortunately, that was not to be the case, with an appeal to the Court of Appeals being flagged almost immediately. Worse was just about to become true – the United Patriots Front was going to hold a rally in Bendigo.

The UPF rally was planned for Saturday, August 29, at the Library Gardens. In the couple of weeks leading up to the rally, many things occurred. Councillor Dinny Adem of the Greater Shepparton City Council invited mosque objectors to tour one of that city's four mosques. The first one built was an Albanian mosque, standing since 1960. Councillor Adem was reported as having said: "I watch what is happening and shake my head..." The mosques are just part of the fabric of Shepparton. Just like anywhere else I might add.

In Bendigo, a large gathering of councillors, State and Federal members for Bendigo, faith leaders and other community leaders met at the Town Hall. They issued a statement in full support of an inclusive and diverse free society. Despite growing rumblings from the objectors, Heri Febriyanto stated that the Muslim community felt overwhelmingly welcome within the city.

As the days ticked by to the UPF rally, anti-racism, left wing groups announced they would be having a counter-rally in Bendigo on the same day. Certainly, local activists helped in all of this – I know some! Melbourne had seen a number of these protests, so nothing was new there. Quite often violent incidents had eventuated. On Wednesday 26th August 2015, police warned the public to stay away from the Bendigo CBD on the coming Saturday, likewise, businesses would be closed as well. Although public safety was a genuine concern, I believe this was a mistake as it gave the UPF an enormous ego boost – "they" had closed Bendigo down. On the eve of the rallies, I saw a simple yet profound message on the cast-iron fence of St Paul's Anglican Cathedral: "PRAY FOR THE PEACE OF BENDIGO".

Saturday 29th August 2015 dawned fairly cold and cloudy, but strangely still. As I walked down Mitchell Street I noted that the normally opened Turkish café was closed. Many other businesses were closed as well, giving central Bendigo an early Sunday morning feel. The numbers of Police were large, and I talked to a few at the water filled plastic barricades around the Library Gardens. They seemed friendly and relaxed. I went over to the Dai Gum San precinct where local greens member, Nathan Wingrave had organised a gathering to promote a respectful, inclusive and diverse Bendigo. There were a couple of dozen people, including children, ranging from families to union and church people in attendance. A BBQ was cooking up loads of free sausages and there was entertainment for the kiddies. I must say that no media was present here, as they were gearing up where the main event was going to be. Over the next three hours, I would roam between the two areas.

The "No Room For Racism" people had originally gathered in Rosalind Park and noisily paraded through what is now William Vahland Place to the Library Gardens. Two main groups were evident – the black flags of the Anarchists and the red flags of the Socialists. I did see Steve Jolly, Socialist Party member and councillor for Yarra City Council. They arrived at the gardens first and the UPF and their supporters then appeared via the Mall. The UPF and supporters held a sea of Australian and kangaroo flags. I would put the anti-mosque crowd at around 200, with their opponents being slightly smaller, say 160. The chanting and roaring was extreme. Talking to a local business owner, who had closed his business for the day, the response I got from him was "This is not Bendigo".

Convicted arsonist and steroid trafficker, Blair Cottrell, UPF leader, spoke before a cheering crowd of loyal supporters. Of the things he said, one clearly sticks in my mind: "If Bendigo gets a mosque, Bendigo will become a caliphate". At that point, one bloke in the front rank forgot where he was and gave a Nazi-like salute. The fact that so many places that had mosques where not caliphates seems to have been lost on the crowd. Bendigo Councillor Elise Chapman was visibly present, wearing an Australian flag like a cape.

On one of my many migrations from the gardens to Dai Gum San and back, I walked past the Hotel Shamrock noting that people were inside having lunch. A tram trundled its way along Pall Mall in amongst passing cars. Quite normal really, but around the corner it was quite abnormal – very ugly in fact.

I did see a scuffle in Lyttleton Terrace between a local youth (I have seen him many times) and anti-racism protesters. The youth had come from the UPF rally and then turned to confront an equally young, partially disguised anarchist, with others then joining in. I was but three metres away from this and then I heard a tremendous sound as UPF members charged the barricades only to be pepper sprayed by the police. Moments later I heard that an Australian flag had been burnt, causing a response from UPF members. A young woman from North Melbourne was later to receive two fines of $600 each for municipal infringements relating to this. Apparently, a UPF member or supporter had been using the pole of the unfurled flag as a prodding weapon, which was seized by the woman concerned.

After a while the anti-racism protestors peeled away, many making for the railway station. About half an hour later the UPF rally broke up, with people heading here and there. Someone told me that both groups were going back to Melbourne on the same train! Sure enough, just before 4.20pm, I saw police all over Bendigo Station, with police in all of the train's carriages. I assume one group was at the front and the other at the back. All non-combatants would have been placed in the middle section.

The whole thing was appalling. Although I admit some sympathies with the anti-racism groups, their attendance gave the UPF just what it wanted, an enormous amount of free publicity. The rallies were reported widely in Australia and overseas, and certainly did nothing to enhance Bendigo as a place to visit or live. It is that simple. Much later, an informant from the local Muslim community told me that the police had instructed Muslims to stay home on the day.

More shocking headlines were made when a Council meeting was shut down on Wednesday 16th September. Anti-mosque protestors "stormed" the meeting, requiring police to escort councillors out of the Town Hall. Julie Hoskin was seen to sit in the Mayoral Chair.

The rumour mill had a field day with all sorts of "facts" being shared on social media. Housing association Haven-Home, Safe was "going to build 20,000 units" to house all the Muslims who were going to arrive in Bendigo, 80,000 people in all! The Council's plan to extend Bendigo Airport was to facilitate the arrival of these Muslims. Other rumours suggested that the Haven CEO Ken Marchingo and Mayor Peter Cox were being bribed by Muslims – all vicious, unfounded and completely untrue. It is to the credit of Bendigo at that very difficult time, that we had in our midst such stalwarts of decency in Ken Marchingo and Peter Cox. We can add to the lengthy list the Advertiser and the Weekly and the may varied community and religious groups as well. Standouts were Bishop Andrew Curnow and Dean John Roundhill of the Anglican Cathedral.

Another UPF rally was announced for Bendigo on Saturday, 10th October 2015. This caused the cancellation of the Bendigo Heritage Uncorked Wine and Food Festival, concurrent with the protest. But not all of Bendigo's residents were going to let political fanaticism ruin Bendigo's otherwise fine reputation – "Believe In Bendigo" was being born.

A group comprising Margot Spaulding, Jayson Tayeh, Damian Wells and many others began organising a family event to showcase Bendigo as a welcoming community. The date set was the very brand new public holiday to celebrate the Australian Football League's Grand Final – Friday, 2nd October 2015. With massive business and local community sponsorship, the Civic Gardens was the scene for a multicultural, community festival – very, very yellow, which was the designated colour for the event. Over the day, a few thousand people took part in the display of multicultural unity.

With the second UPF rally, a notable novelty was the International Junk Orchestra at Railway Place. Organised by local artists, a small group of people made improvised music on improvised instruments, including saucepans, in support of multiculturalism.

The second rally, highly organised by the police, saw the UPF marshalling at the Forest and Mackenzie Street intersection before marching to Rosalind Park. The anti-racism protestors held a rally at the Library Gardens before marching to Sidney Myer Place. The footbridge between the two was filled with police. It was a very warm 30 degree day and very much "same old, same old". One beautiful thing I recall was when I came up behind the UPF, at some distance, and followed them down Mackenzie Street. From the old hotel on the corner of View Street, John Lennon's "Imagine" was blaring out of a stereo from the balcony, with two young teenage girls slowly dancing to it. Below, the T-shirted UPF members and supporters chanted "Aussie, Aussie, Aussie, Oi ,Oi, Oi". Talk about Beauty and the Beast.

The last UPF rally took place in early 2016. The Court of Appeals would uphold the Council's approval of a mosque in Bendigo, with the opponents applying to the High Court of Australia for yet another costly appeal. In time, the High Court would dismiss the application, with local resident and mosque objector Julie Hoskin facing hefty legal costs.

At the next Council elections, most of the former council members would not be re-elected, including Elise Chapman and Helen Leach who had voted against the mosque. Councillors Campbell and Ruffel did not seek re-election. Julie Hoskin was elected as a councillor for the Whipstick Ward but would resign during her first and only term on Council.

The Bendigo Islamic Community Centre is slowly being built and Bendigo has returned to its former glorious self. I salute those councillors who stood their ground in the name of human decency, at what was a very difficult time for all. I wonder what has happened to those 80,000 Muslims that were meant to have descended upon Bendigo? Must have got on the wrong plane, I guess. Haven has yet to build 20,000 units here – I am sure they would love to as it would create much needed affordable housing. And, as a postscript, on Australian Day 2018, the UPF held a rally at the Moreland City Council. Only seven people showed up.

CHAPTER NINETEEN

A VERY BENDIGO WELCOME.

The story of human culture in the City of Greater Bendigo began with the Dja Dja Wurrung and Taungurung people. They are part of a rich tapestry of First Nation culture spanning the continent and quite different to, say, First Nation cultures of the western and northern parts of the country. Tasmanian First Nation people are diverse as well. Having survived the violent shock of invasion and attempts to fully assimilate them, their ancient culture remains strong.

In November 2013, the Victorian Government recognised the Dja Wurrung people as the traditional owners of Country. This was a breakthrough in native title rights. Some original owners found themselves employed as Rangers in Parks Victoria, in an effort to bring ancient local wisdom and strategies into managing forests and water supplies, amongst other things. With the construction of a world class theatre at the former Bendigo Goal in 2016, the name Ulumbarra was chosen, which means meeting or gathering place. The Ravenswood interchange development saw two old, deceased scar trees removed and placed outside the Ulumbarra Theatre, the scars having been cut by ancestors for either shields or to carry seeds or ochre.

April 2016 saw the Council adopt its Reconciliation Plan, further promoting cultural awareness, employment opportunities and an integration of local and regional art into exhibitions at the Bendigo Art Gallery.

The Autumn of 2017 saw a return of traditional methods of fire management in regional forests – the first time in 170 years to be precise. The very slow mosaic burns give good fire breaks, while leaving islands of vegetation unharmed. Quite different to the damaging scorched earth policies usually regarded as normal practice. In August 2017, a Dja Dja Wurrung Tram took to the rails to promote local traditional culture – quite possibly a world first.

We still have a long way to go for full reconciliation, but certainly progress has been made since the beginning of this new century.

During the last decade of so, Bendigo has really experienced an arrival of people from the four corners of the globe. This is perhaps greater than the 1850's, given that most arrivals then were European or Chinese. We've seen a second wave of Chinese arrive recently, although from many parts of China and not just the south as once upon a time. We have people arriving from our near neighbours to the north and from Africa. The Indian population of Bendigo has seen steady growth and once again displays a diversity of culture within the sub-continent. The local Sikh community has expressed a desire to build a temple, but no formal plans have yet been developed. We have small populations of people from the Americas and the Middle East, all coming together to call Bendigo home. Most have come as migrants, just as the ancestors of long term Bendigonians families once were – unless they arrived in chains on a convict ship! Some have come as refugees, fleeing conflict and persecution to start life afresh in a safer location.

Of the refuges, the Karen people of Myanmar (Burma) are the most numerous of those seeking asylum. Now numbering over 2,000, the Karen population of Bendigo comprise both Buddhist and various Christian denominations, with most coming from refugee camps in Thailand. To give you an idea of what they experienced in Myanmar, I quote directly from a document supplied by the Bendigo Community Health Services. Although it details the Karen experience, such experiences are common to other people seeking asylum. "Communities report trauma and torture including beatings, slappings, kicking, maiming, breaking bones, being bound or tied up, stress to the senses, deprivation of medical treatment, forced labour, rape, psychological abuse, asphyxiation, slavery, electric shock, burning, death, removal of eyes, exposure to extreme heat or cold. In addition, the Karen people have been impacted in many cases by restricted access to food and water and the widespread use of landmines." Unfortunately, there are some people in our community who feel that refugees should not be allowed into our country.

In 2017, the Bendigo Chinese Association announced that Sun Loong would have to be retired. The funds for a new dragon, to be named Dai Gum Loong, Big Gold Dragon, were sought through public and corporate donations and grants from three tiers of government.

A huge shift in traditional aspects of culture was made with the plebiscite on Same Sex Marriages in the Spring of 2017. Until the 1980's it was illegal for gay men to engage in sexual activity, but a rise in campaigns for human equality and diversity would overturn the old laws. In the postal survey for Marriage Equality, Bendigo returned a YES vote of 68.7%.

In the course of the research for this book, I spoke with elected representatives of Bendigo, both in the State and Federal parliaments. All three were women at the time of interview, which was a new milestone for Bendigo. In order of being elected we have Jacinta Allan, Member for Bendigo East; Maree Edwards, Member for Bendigo West; and Lisa Chesters, Federal Member for Bendigo. I asked them for their opinions regarding the strengths and challenges of a multicultural Bendigo.

Jacinta Allan sees it as continuing our history, with waves of migrants building the foundation of modern Bendigo, including the Chinese cultural link. The growth of health and other services was attracting specialists and practitioners from around the world. Multiculturalism also creates new jobs and other activities that can promote tourism. Ms Allan saw some challenges as being the need to recognise that most people are warm and welcoming here. She stated that there was a need to be vigilant and aware of people who felt threatened and left behind by change. It is the responsibility of leaders to help the process of integration and participation in a non-exclusive way. Ms Allan voiced concern over social media, stating that "it is used like a megaphone" to the vulnerable.

Maree Edwards stated that most people in her electorate could trace their family back to other countries and faiths. A great supporter of the

Great Stupa, Ms Edwards sees it as promoting Bendigo as an attractive place for all faiths and cultures. An increase in people taking Australian Citizenship is seen as a plus for Bendigo and the country as a whole. Ms Edwards said that many issues based on global events and misconceptions, such as Muslims and Islam, stem from fear and ignorance. Bendigo can stand together as a welcoming and diverse community. Ms Edwards doesn't see much of a challenge in multiculturalism itself, rather population growth does create strains on vital infrastructure and services, which do need to be addressed. Ms Edwards sees a need for Bendigo leadership to be driven by people who appreciate difference.

Lisa Chesters sees multiculturalism as a great way to tell out stories, with our shared Easter Festival bringing people together. It gives us a vibrant community and a diverse job market, growing our diversity. Ms Chesters also thought that inclusiveness positively challenges us when it comes to faith, music, food and dance from a variety of cultures. Also, Bendigo can offer a safe and inclusive space, whereas big cities can cause a loss of community. In terms of challenges, Ms Chester sees education playing a vital role here as well as honesty. There is a need to call out lies and misconceptions about people from different cultures and faiths, especially concerns about "who's taking your job?". Ms Chesters saw it important to rebuild Bendigo's reputation and that we needed to be mature in how we use social media.

And what a difference is now underway in Bendigo! As people settle, they start to showcase their many and varied talents. Just as Melbourne has a fine reputation for global food, Bendigo is gaining a reputation for food as well. Many people are now organising their own cultural festivals and this will surely grow over the years to come. In case anyone thinks that the Anglo-Celtic population has been squeezed out of things, the Scots Day Out in Bendigo is a recent great example of celebrating the Celtic component of traditional Aussie culture. The haggis has returned to Bendigo once more!

In May 2018, the Stupa's Festival of Light became Illumin 8 – and the well-travelled Jade Buddha made its triumphant return to Myer's Flat after nine years abroad. Some 10,000 people attended the rather colossal event.

The Easter Festival of 2019 saw a record crowd of 80,000 people line View Street, Pall Mall, McCrae and Chapel Streets to witness the arrival of the new Imperial Dragon – Dai Gum Loong. The enormous Big Gold Dragon, with its massive head and 120 metre long body was taking over from Sun Loong, who needed a restoration. All four imperial Dragons were present, Sun Loong, Yar Loong, Dai Gum Loong and Loong for the transition ceremony, which took place at the Alexandria Fountain. An expected delay in the Easter Procession was exacerbated when Loong required some repairs in View Street – the ageing silk thread in its body started to break, requiring immediate restitching with new silk thread. An amazing spectacle probably never to be repeated, as Loong has proven that fragility was well advanced.

Times have changed in the new 21st century. A century before Chinese, Indian and other non-European immigration had been curtailed. With the arrival of Dai Gum Loong, accompanied by a Lion team from the dragon maker in Hong Kong, Bendigo residents gathered with Australian and newer Australian people to welcome the new dragon into a truly multicultural society.

CHAPTER TWENTY

THE TRIUMPH OF THE DRAGON.

When Australia closed its door to most of the world in 1901, it also closed the door to a range of new possibilities. That door creaked open in the 1940's, allowing greater diversity in experiencing and expressing the wonderment of being human. Despite non-British people arriving in large numbers, the Anglo fabric of society remained intact. It became very normal to go to the footy on a Saturday afternoon and then have a pizza for dinner, or Chinese, or Souvlaki. The sky didn't fall in, if you take a look.

Bendigo swam against the tide until the arrival of this brand-new century, when people from around the world began to arrive and add more than a splash of colour to the local landscape. Unlike places like Ballarat and Beechworth, Bendigo was able to keep a population of Chinese descendants of those from the roaring 1850's. And where would Bendigo be without its dragons? As much as the Chinese were feared for their difference, local residents made the Chinese contingent of the Easter Procession the most eagerly awaited and appreciated. There can be great joy in experiencing cultural difference, even if we don't fully understand it.

Just as the great forests of the world display great diversity – in fact it makes up the dynamic of a forest and the planet – humans have built up their own diversity over thousands of centuries. It would be a dull old world if everyone ate Chiko Rolls and barracked for Collingwood. Diversity is a natural part of the order of things, ever changing and ever expanding.

Certainly, worldwide as well as here, there are those who are fearful of the "stranger", someone who looks, sounds, believes in ways that seem quite foreign to our own long held perspectives. This is a problem when we automatically conclude that this is a threat to us. I am very aware that most bushrangers of over a century ago were either Irish born or had Irish parents. At the time, people did not fear the Irish people as potentially being a bushranger. Indeed, some of those at the receiving end of a bushranger's bullet were Irish themselves, just think of Ned Kelly and the three police shot at Stringy Bark Creek, Lonegan, Scanlon and Kennedy.

Diversity is part of the natural order, but acceptance comes slowly to some members of the human race. And it is not a case of Anglos versus everyone else. It is simply a fear of the unknown, quite often with fear being broken down to False Evidence Appearing Real. Any fear can block us from experiencing our full potential, both individually and collectively.

At this point in human history, we really do need to start pulling together as we face problems caused by us and us alone – climate change, mountains of toxic waste, fouling of waterways and seas, overcrowded cities and an increasing gap in those who have plenty and those who go without. It is as if our communal home is on fire and we are at each other's throats arguing about the furniture.

Not much use pointing the finger at "them" because it all starts and ends with that most difficult of human beings – me. The reality is: one very diverse humanity on one very diverse planet. It's that simple. As a respectful and joyous multicultural society, Bendigo can experience the world right outside the front door, which is much the same as what happens in Melbourne and elsewhere.

I'll leave you with the greatest of all Aussie blessings: Goodonyer!

CREDITS

The Age

The Bendigo Advertiser,

Bendigo Weekly,

Bendigo Independent

Bendigonian

Heri Febriyanto and the Bendigo Islamic Association

Bendigo Historical Society

The Bendigo Trust

Golden Dragon Museum

National Library of Australia (Trove)

Goldfields Library (Bendigo)

Bendigo Action Coalition/Collective

Colin King

Rodney Carter, Dja Dja Wurrung Clans Corporation

Loddon Campaspe Multicultural Service

Bendigo Community Health Services

Terry Davidson: "Jewish Worship in Bendigo (Sandhurst)", Bendigo Historical Society 2017

Frank Cusack: "Bendigo, A History" (Revised Edition) Lerk and McClure 2006

George Mackay: "History of Bendigo", Lerk and McClure 2000

Bilal Cleland:" The Muslims in Australia – A Brief History", Islamic Council of Victoria 2002

John Safran: "Depends What You Mean By Extremist", Penguin/Hamish Hamilton 2017

The many diverse people I have spoken to or have eavesdropped on.

ABOUT THE AUTHOR

Bill Clyde is a history buff and a born teacher, with a gift for making history come to life. Researching and writing the story of Bendigo's many peoples and influences has been a remarkable journey of Bill.

Bill hopes readers also enjoy the journey.